"Gone But not Forgotten.."
In memory of you
LADY who made ..
"Happy Fathers D
The Keiths, T.
the Hagoods" ✓

Enjoy !!!

The Epitome of Fatherhood

The Life of Chester M. Whittaker

Thank you for
the support!!

Thank you for
the support!!

[signature]

The Epitome of Fatherhood

The Life of Chester M. Whittaker

Celeste E. Whittaker

AHLP Books
Cherry Hill, New Jersey

AHLP Books, an imprint of Africana Homestead Legacy Publishers Inc.
811 Church Road, Suite 105
Cherry Hill, NJ 08002 USA
www.ahlpub.com

Library of Congress Cataloging-in-Publication Data

Whittaker, Celeste.
The epitome of fatherhood : the life of Chester M. Whittaker / Celeste Whittaker.
     p. cm.
Includes bibliographical references and index.
Summary: "Using the subject's private papers, oral interviews, and the author's
recollections, presents Chester M. Whittaker's childhood and college years in North
Carolina and Virginia and his life as a family man, educator, coach, community
leader, and church leader in New Jersey"--Provided by publisher.
ISBN 978-0-9818939-4-5 (pbk. : alk. paper)
1. Whittaker, Chester M., 1933-1997. 2. Fathers--United States--Biography.
3. Fathers and daughters--United States. 4. Whittaker, Celeste--Childhood and
youth. 5. Whitaker family. I. Title.
CT275.W5554W48 2009
929'.20973--dc22
                              2009034349

Photo credits: Photographs courtesy of Dolores E. Whittaker, Clarence E.
Whittaker, Sr., and the author.

Contents

Preface   vii

Acknowledgments   xi

Chapter 1 Chester "Junior"   1
   Family and early childhood   1
   Summers in North Carolina   4

Chapter 2 Growing Up   7
   College years in Petersburg, Virginia   8

Chapter 3 Life in New Jersey   11
   From Fort Dix to the classroom   11
   A romance changes Dad's life   11

Chapter 4 Growing Family   15

Chapter 5 Job in the Midwest   19

Chapter 6 Back in New Jersey   21
   Settling in Willingboro   21
   Coaching a daughter in basketball   21

Chapter 7 Oh, Brother   25

Chapter 8 Newport News and the Farm   29
   Vacationing in Newport News, Virginia   29

Chapter 9 Taking Celeste to College   33

Chapter 10 Dad the Pioneer   41
   Education and government service   41
   Awards for excellence and service   44

Chapter 11 A Helping Hand   47

Chapter 12 The Power Multiplied   51

Chapter 13 The Call   55

Chapter 14 The Day   63

Chapter 15 Daddy's Girls Remember Him   69

Chapter 16 The Grands   77

Chapter 17 Remember Whose Hands You're In   81

Epilogue The Epitome of Fatherhood   83

Bibliography   85

Index   87

About the Author   99

Preface

My dad was my hero, pure and simple. Chester M. Whittaker was truly an example of what a father, husband, brother, son, uncle and nephew should be.

This book is dedicated to my dad, the late Chester M. Whittaker. It's been twelve years since his death and it is still unbelievable to me that this vivacious man is gone. But, as a poem I once read for him stated, he was the epitome of fatherhood.

Another reason for this book is the fact that my dad put a scrapbook together years ago about his life. In the front of the scrapbook, he wrote: My Book....By Chet Whittaker. He also wrote these words:

> The pictures, letters, programs, and memories were updated in September of 1991. By far, it does not include every facet of my life; however, it does focus on some significant aspects of my years on this earth. I trust that with the tender love of my wife Dolores and my sweet daughters, that it may inspire some young person to strive to be a better person.
>
> Years after my death, I hope that it will say to those who turn the pages that I loved, lived and tried to help people.

I wrote this book to leave a legacy for his children, grandchildren, great-grandchildren and great-great grandchildren. Years from now someone can read this and have some clue, some inkling, about who this wonderful man was. Everyone should have been lucky enough to know him for themselves, but at least maybe through my words, they will get a small glimpse into who our Daddy really was.

He was a fantastic man, and I will miss him forever. One of the biggest things he showed me, as a woman, is how a woman should be treated by a man. There was no disrespect or disregard for my mother. He loved her, and he wasn't afraid to show us or her that he did. My mom had happy memories of him to share:

> He just believed in celebrating all the time. He always gave me flowers. He always remembered birthdays, holidays, Valentine's Day, Mother's Day. He was always giving. Giving, giving, giving. I'd say, 'It's Valentine's Day, please

don't get me any candy.' He'd get it any way. He just felt it was something he had to do. He never, ever forgot my birthday. He always did something special for my birthday.

It was great that he never had to be reminded. He would always give me something special. He just wanted me to have things. He treated me special, he really did. He was crazy about his mother. He just worshiped his mother and his father, too. But his mother was just special to him.

This book is for anyone who has ever had a father, a real father. It doesn't matter if the person is a blood relative, as long as they nurture you, care for you and show you nothing but unconditional love and support. That is what a father is. A father is—

- someone who is a constant in your life and a consistent example of what a real man should be.
- someone who provides for you and protects you from harm.
- someone who would literally give you their last breath if they could.
- someone who is always there for you, even when you act the fool.
- someone who tells you, you are somebody, and they really, really mean it.
- someone who pushes you towards your dreams and goals, even when you sometimes doubt yourself.
- someone who allows you to love them, too, and revels in the little trinkets and thoughtful gifts that you give them, just because it's from you.
- someone who's not afraid to hug you or show you affection, because they know children need to be hugged.

I asked my mom recently what she missed the most about my dad. She said,

Everything. Just him being here. What can I say? I just can't believe he's gone. I still have to remember he's not here. I know it's been [twelve] years, but it doesn't seem like it. It seems like it just happened, really. I can still feel [him]. I guess he's always here with me, I guess that's the reason.

I know that he is with me and that he's watching over me. I wouldn't have gotten this far if it wasn't for him. I just miss everything. We always were together. Family came first with him, everything was family. He wasn't a person who got involved with other stuff. In later years, once we joined St. John, the only thing that would take him away would be the church. Working at the center, going there every night. But it's something he enjoyed doing. I couldn't take that away from him. He didn't do anything else. He wasn't one who would go to football games all the time, or basketball games. He liked to watch TV. But when he wasn't at the church, he was home.

Acknowledgments

First and foremost, I would like to thank God for allowing me to complete this project, and for allowing me to have a father like I was blessed to have. There were times when I didn't feel like I could write it. As a friend pointed out to me, perhaps it was because I felt by completing it, it was like letting go of Dad. That maybe I wouldn't have as much of a reason to think or talk about him.

I would like to thank my entire family, starting with my mom, for choosing a great Dad for us girls, and for being a strong woman, who was actually more of the backbone of the family than we ever knew. She let Dad be Dad. I could write a book about her being the "Epitome of Motherhood", because she is that. She's a wonderful, loving, generous, loyal, thoughtful person, who gives love to her family so freely. Thanks Mom for all your help with the book, and for being a wonderful example to all of us!

I would like to thank all my sisters—Saundra, Shelly, Anna, and Monica —as well as my brothers-in-law, Pierre and Travis, for their belief in me, encouragement, love, support and prayers! Shelly also did my makeup for my picture. I would also like to thank all my nieces and nephews for your love and for being an inspiration for the book.

To Uncle Clarence, Aunt Liz, and all my cousins, and all my other relatives who have prayed for me and encouraged me, I also say thanks. Uncle provided me with a lot of information for the book, through many anecdotes, and comments about Dad. Aunt Clarkie and Cousin Sis also provided insight. My cousin Clarence also read over my contract from Africana Homestead Legacy Publishers and gave me the approval.

I thank my friends, Nina Jones (who helped me have my breakthrough), Kathy Wilson Duprey, Sharon Byrd, Crystal Tucker, Jason Curry, Mike Drake, Bill Barksdale, and Cathy Wood (who also did my hair for my bio picture) for encouraging me to always go after my dreams and for lovingly supporting me in those dreams. I would also be remiss if I did not thank Rev. Norris and Rev. Townsend for their brilliant insight and prayers through this process. They were so loved and respected by my dad, and the feeling was clearly mutual. They were also instrumental in his spiritual growth, which eventually led him to the ministry.

I also have to thank the late Westry Horne, for the example he set for my dad, and for all the stories and wisdom he shared with me before his passing. The entire Horne family – the late Mrs. Dorothy Horne, as well as Jackie and

Judi, in particular – have supported me greatly through this process, with feedback, encouragement and prayers.

I thank Jeanne West, whom I met in a car dealership in South Jersey, and who led me to the path of Africana Homestead Legacy Publishers Inc. by making the introduction to the publisher, and, finally, I'd like to thank Carolyn C. Williams, president and chief operating officer at AHLP, for giving an unknown, first-time author a chance to live her dream, and to leave a legacy for Chester Whittaker's family. I would also like to thank Denise Henhoeffer, a *Courier-Post* colleague, for taking my photograph.

Because of you all, future generations will have the opportunity to read about this wonderful man, and get a slight glimpse into who he was! Last but not least, I thank my dad, Chester M. Whittaker, for being the Epitome of Fatherhood. I will love you forever!

Chapter 1
Chester "Junior"

Family and early childhood

My dad, Chester Mack Whitaker (which he later spelled Whittaker), was born on November 25, 1933, in Tarboro, North Carolina, to Chester Whitaker and Hazel Lee (née Kearney) Whitaker who had married on December 25, 1932. His dad, like his grandfather, Roswell Whitaker, was a self-employed farmer. His mother who was beautiful, tall, and slim well into her eighties was born in Tarboro, North Carolina, and attended public school in Edgecombe County, North Carolina. To earn money, she worked for a family in Tarboro. According to his father's sister, Clarkie (née Whitaker) Lyons, Dad was born on the McNair Farm between Tarboro and Leggett, North Carolina, in a small tenant house where his father was a sharecropper. In 1934 Dad's father moved the family back to his grandparents home (also in Tarboro) to help them, after his father's brother, Jefferson, was killed in a car accident at the age of eighteen.

Tarboro, according to the town's Web site, was founded in 1760. The ninth oldest incorporated town in North Carolina, it served as a very important colonial river port and a thriving trade center until the Civil War. Located in Edgecombe County, it is also known as the town where President George Washington slept during a visit in his 1791 tour of the South. President Washington reportedly said, "it was the best salute you could have from a single cannon." Tarboro was originally known as Tawboro, then Tarrburg, then, in 1760, was chartered as Tarborough. Located about sixty-eight miles east of Raleigh, North Carolina, it is situated on the bank of the Tar River.

Since Dad had the same first name as his father, and although his middle name was Mack, his parents quickly called him "Junior," a name his family called him for the rest of his life. My dad looked like his father and his paternal grandfather, Reverend Roswell Whitaker. He was light-skinned, very handsome, even in his youth, had a distinctive mole over his left eye, and had ears that slightly protruded when he was a young boy.

Nearly four years after Dad was born, his brother, Clarence Edward, was born. Dad and Uncle Clarence were as close as brothers could be. They loved each other very much and were proud of each other. They looked alike, although his brother had a darker complexion and was slimmer than Dad. Uncle Clarence called Dad "Junior," and my dad often called Uncle Clarence

"Brother." When still youngsters, they both changed the spelling of their last name and stuck with that choice throughout their lives.

After living in Tarboro a short time, Dad's family moved to a house at 1033 32nd Street in Newport News, Virginia, on the city's east side. Newport News, Virginia, is located where the James River and Chesapeake Bay meet and runs about twenty-five miles along the James River and Hampton Roads Harbor. According to the city's official Web site, Newport News was named for Christopher Newport, who was captain of the Susan Constant, the lead ship of the three that carried the Jamestown settlers to the new world in 1607. Since the turn of the 19th century, it's been known as the provider of the nation's finest, technologically advanced military ships.

After the family settled in Newport News, Dad's mother was employed by the Newport News public school system—often working in the school cafeteria. She retired after more than twelve years of service. Dad's father worked at the Newport News shipyard and for the U.S. Postal Service, among other places. Real handy, he could build additions onto houses and other types of things, although he had no formal training in carpentry. Chester Senior could do electrical work as well. Dad's father and mother raised their boys in a strict,

Above: Hazel Lee (née Kearney) Whitaker, my dad's mother, n.d. Below: Chester Whitaker, Sr., my dad's father, n.d.

Hazel and Chester Whitaker, Sr., n.d.

Christian household. Since Dad's grandfather was a preacher that was not surprising.

When Dad's family moved into their house at 1033 32nd Street in Newport News, it was a one-bedroom house on one floor, and he and his brother often slept in the living room. With his construction skills, his father transformed the house into a two-story, three-bedroom house with many other improvements. First, he added a room onto the back of the house. In later years, he added the second story and a den in the back.

The Whitaker home at 1033 32nd Street in Newport News, Virginia. With his construction skills, Dad's father renovated their one-floor, one-bedroom house into this two-story house with three bedrooms to provide a more spacious home for their family, n.d.

People were impressed with the changes to that home over the years. It was a white with green shutters. Although it had a small front yard, Dad's father kept everything neatly trimmed. And there was a birdbath out front. In the back yard, they had a covered porch that was separate from the house. The family sat outside in the porch in the summer, eating sliced watermelon or just talking and laughing. It was honestly one of the prettiest houses on the block.

Although they didn't get much formal education and neither attended high school, Chester Senior and Hazel were determined to educate their sons. During those years, the schools in Newport News like the rest of Virginia were segregated. Dad and his brother attended Booker T. Washington Elementary School on Chestnut Avenue from first grade to eighth grade, and they attended Huntington High School (officially, the Collis Porter Huntington High School), right down the street from their house. (Huntington High School is notable for producing former Secretary of Energy Hazel O'Leary, who became president of Fisk University in 2004. When we visited as young children, we often walked down the street to the track at Huntington High School.)

My dad was always talkative, outgoing, and filled with humor. As a youngster, he was active in school sports and was very active socially. His warm, loving personality never changed throughout his life.

Even as a boy, Dad loved to dress well. When he was in middle school, he would have his mom iron five or six shirts for him. He would lay the shirts out on the bed, trying to figure out which recently-pressed shirt he would wear that day. Sometimes, he would even go to the five and ten store and buy another shirt. His mother told people how he would sometimes come home from school and change his crisply ironed white shirt into another one, if that first shirt was the least bit dirty. She bought him nice slacks, because he didn't like jeans. My uncle Clarence said that Dad was inspired to dress well by members of the Whitaker and Kearney families. Their parents who occasionally won the local Easter Parade were role models, as were their uncles—Uncle Fate Kearney, Uncle Lewis Kearney, and Uncle Birt Whitaker. Dad was dressing sharp at an early age, and he carried that on through high school, college, and the rest of his life.

Very popular with people, young and old, my dad was probably the most popular kid in his neighborhood, according to his brother. Back in the 1950's in Newport News, Dad had the only basketball net around, and every boy in the neighborhood came to his house every day to play. He was good at basketball back then. Uncle Clarence used to watch, mostly, since he was four years younger than Dad and most of Dad's friends.

Summers in North Carolina

While still children, Dad and Uncle Clarence spent many summers in Tarboro or Whitakers, North Carolina, visiting relatives, including their paternal grandfather, Reverend Roswell Whitaker. All of their relatives in North Carolina used to love for them to visit, especially because Dad was fun-loving and led many of their activities. He was an extrovert, always smiling and teasing his younger cousins. His grandfather had an apple tree, and all of the cousins played house under it. Dad made the rules, and the young cousins had to follow him. From about age ten or eleven he also took part in their "preaching contests" where his love of preaching truly began. Usually, he was the winner.

Spending summers in North Carolina let Dad also grow up with Birt Whitaker, his uncle. Birt who was Chester Senior's baby brother was only a few years older than young Chester. When Dad was in his early teens, he and Birt helped prepare the green tobacco for curing and for sale at the auction sales on the market.

My dad reminisced about having the opportunity to visit his grandfather Roswell's farm and to work in the tobacco fields each summer while speaking at his uncle Birt's funeral in 1995. "As a youngster who spent many summers in Tarboro and Whitakers, North Carolina, I had the rare opportunity of growing up with Uncle Birt, to a large extent. I loved to go to Granddaddy Whitaker's farm each summer and work in tobacco."

In his remarks, Dad told how his Uncle Birt helped teach him to drive a tobacco truck and how they raced the trucks back to the farm where they would often be scolded by Granddaddy Roswell. He also spoke about how his Uncle Birt organized preaching contests and how he competed against other relatives or some of his uncle's friends. The contests were held under the big tree in the side yard of the farm. Because many of his other cousins visited in the summers as well, one would imagine many lessons were learned out there in the fields.

Family members who shared stories about the time they spent with "Junior," as they called my dad, at the family farm had similar memories of him. Clarkie (née Whitaker) Lyons, his aunt, and Doris (née Lyons) Jones, his cousin, remembered his sense of humor very well. To them he was always "jolly, and making you laugh at his jokes."

Aunt Clarkie, Cousin Doris, and Uncle Clarence also remembered nicknames that my dad gave to people. Dad called his mom either Momma or "Hay," short for Hazel, and he called her younger sister, Florence Brown, "Aunt Sister." He called Granddaddy "Law," because Dad's father always asked a lot of questions and checked out every story that "Junior" used to tell. Some of the nicknames that he gave to his first cousins were "Sonny Boy" (William Brown, son of Aunt Florence Brown, Hazel Whitaker's sister), "Bubba" (Theodore Brown, also a son of Aunt Florence Brown), "Smook" (William Kearney, son of Uncle Richard and Aunt Eula Kearney), "Bo" and "Brother Bill" (Royster Leon Whitaker, son of Uncle Royster Whitaker, Chester Whitaker, Sr.'s, brother).

My dad's first cousins, William "Smook" Kearney and Cousin Eula (née Kearney) Richardson, were actually double cousins. Their mother, Aunt Eula (née Whitaker) Kearney, was his father's sister, and their father, Uncle Richard Kearney, was his mother's brother.

Dad, Cousin Eula, also called "Cousin Sis," and Uncle Clarence often played together, rode bicycles, and walked in the tobacco patches during the summertime. They were pretty close when they were growing up. Over the years, Eula and my dad called themselves closer than brother and sister. The cousins looked forward to seeing each other when staying with Granddaddy Roswell.

Dad and Eula really were like brother and sister, particularly after she lost her brother in a tragic roadside accident, which was later investigated by the authorities. William (Smook) who was in the Marines died the day before his twenty-first birthday, while on his way back to Camp Lejeune, North Carolina. Family members found his body on the side of the highway with tire marks across his chest. People speculated that he must have passed out or been hit on the head, and must have been lying on the highway when a car ran across him. His death was followed years later by another family tragedy, when Dad's cousin, Ray Allen, was killed in a truck wreck. Ray was the son of my dad's Aunt Arrillear (née Kearney) Allen, Nana's sister, whom we called Aunt Teentsy.

Eula, too, remembered "Junior" being a jokester, always up to playing a prank, and always teasing as a child. She said his personality made it a lovely time just being around him.

That was my dad. Being around so many different family members as a young boy allowed him to feel comfortable around just about anybody. And that quality allowed him to have success later in his life. During those years of visiting the farm, his personality developed. He was very outgoing and loved spending time with his extended family members.

Chapter 2
Growing Up

At Huntington High School, Dad was voted "most popular" in the class. He was on the basketball team, and belonged to the math club and choir. In his senior year, he also did some radio broadcasting with the English department.

Chester Whittaker, my dad, in high school: above, back row, sixth from left; below, right.

English Department Broadcast Over WGH

When he was growing up, Dad's parents sometimes worked two jobs at the same time. His father worked for people in the neighborhood, at times, cutting lawns and doing other odd jobs. One family whom he worked for was the Jobes who lived nearby, and Dad's father took Dad with him to help work. One day, showing his own mind, my dad came home and said, "Momma, I'm not going over the Jobes with Daddy anymore." His father later said he had asked Dad to actually work (probably meaning that he wanted my dad to show more effort). Maybe his father had pushed him a little hard. Granddaddy said he would never ask my dad to go back with him, and he kept his word. Instead, Uncle Clarence went to work at the Jobes's with their father, and he did a fine job.

Since their parents worked so much, Dad and his brother were responsible for a lot of the household chores. Although Dad had a very strong work ethic that he inherited from his mother and father, he also knew how to delegate if he needed to. Uncle Clarence told a funny story to that end. When Dad was about fourteen or fifteen, he had a girlfriend whom he got to come and clean up the house. But his parents thought the boys were doing an excellent job cleaning. Despite this trick, Dad's work ethic carried him on through college and after.

College years in Petersburg, Virginia

After graduating high school, my dad attended Virginia State College in nearby Petersburg, Virginia. Since his family had very little money, he probably would not have gone to college without help from a member of their community. As a youngster, Dad was acquainted with most of the influential black leaders in Newport News, including Otis Smith, who owned the local funeral home which still exists and is run by Mr. Smith's son. Otis Smith gave my dad a scholarship to help him attend college.

Dad also worked part-time to help pay his tuition. One of his first jobs ever was running an elevator at Randall H. Hagner & Company Realtors in Washington, District of Columbia in the summers. He was living with his Uncle Fate Kearney in Washington, D.C., at that time.

Otis Smith was a member of the Alpha Phi Alpha Fraternity, Inc., and he influenced Dad to pledge and become an Alpha, and Dad influenced his brother, Uncle Clarence, who attended Morgan State College to become an Alpha. Dad was proud to be an Alpha, and he helped many people throughout his life like other men who belonged to the fraternity. The Alpha Phi Alpha Fraternity, Inc., was formed on December 4, 1906, on the campus of Cornell University in Ithaca, New York, and was the first intercollegiate fraternity established by African Americans. Well over 185,000 men have been initiated into the fraternity which evolved into a primarily service organization. The seven founders of Alpha Phi Alpha are referred to as the "Seven Jewels" and some of its most famous members have been the Reverend Dr. Martin Luther King, Jr., Thurgood Marshall, former Supreme Court justice, Andrew Young, former Atlanta mayor and United Nations ambassador, Maynard Jackson, former Atlanta mayor, Jesse Owens, Olympic gold medalist in track and field, and many others.

Because he loved basketball, my dad played on his college team. One of his teammates at Virginia State was a man by the name of Adam Wade (born Patrick Henry Wade) who went on to fame as a singer, actor, first black game show host, director, writer, and producer (bio from an interview given to the *HistoryMakers*, April 27, 2007).

Chester Whittaker, my dad, as a member of the basketball team at Virginia State College in Petersburg, Virginia.

At Virginia State my dad still loved to dress well. He was so stylish that he had J. B. Sanders, a close friend and tailor whom he met in college, to make his clothes. Dad took pride in his clothes his whole life. He didn't worry much about other material things, but he loved having a nice suit made every year. After he graduated, Dad ordered a few suits from J. B. every year.

Dad didn't necessarily feel that clothes made the man, but he just loved to look nice and smell good.

Chester Whittaker, my dad, in his twenties, being cool. He loved to dress in fine suits, n.d.

That was his thing. He knew that a man wearing a nice suit and a pair of good-looking shoes attracts people's attention. And Dad could get anyone's attention. He was charismatic.

Family members sometimes teased my dad because even on the weekends, he would wear a nice pair of slacks and a nice shirt or even a suit and tie. He just wasn't a casual kind of person.

Career advice has told people to dress for the position that they want, not necessarily for the position they already have. In other words, if people work at a company in the mail room, they can still wear nice slacks and a tie for work, because, ultimately, they may aspire to work in customer service or marketing or some other department within the company. In other words, dress for success. Dad showed this type of pride in his attire from his boyhood.

While still at Virginia State, Dad was accepted into the *Reserve Officers' Training Corps* (*ROTC*), a college-based, officer commissioning program. He completed his training at the ROTC Summer Camp in Fort Meade, Maryland, in the summer of 1955. With a B.S. degree in recreational therapy and his Army commission, he moved to New Jersey.

Chapter 3
Life in New Jersey

From Fort Dix to the classroom

After graduating from college, Dad was commissioned as an officer in the Army at Fort Dix, New Jersey, on November 7, 1958. Besides carrying out his military duties, my dad coached basketball, and his team won the championship in 1959. Dad was a first lieutenant and received citations for his work with the sports teams. He served as officer-in-charge of the post baseball team as well. Promoted to the rank of captain, Dad received an honorable discharge from the Army in August 1966.

By the time he was stationed at Fort Dix, Dad was married to his first wife (January 1955) and had a young daughter, my sister Saundra. To supplement his Army pay, he worked nights at a local Howard Johnson's washing dishes to support his family and to make ends meet. But his marriage did not work out.

After Dad and his first wife separated, he rented a room from Bernice Roy, an elderly lady who lived in Moorestown, New Jersey. At that time Dad taught special education at the William R. Allen School in Burlington City and coached track and field at the high school. The William R. Allen School was a segregated school that was built for black children in 1900.

A romance changes Dad's life

Little did my dad know, but his life was about to change again. He no-

Chester Whittaker, my dad, coaching his Army basketball team at Fort Dix, New Jersey. At the time of this photo, it was a United States Army Training Center, Infantry Army base. Today, Fort Dix is a major training and mobilization center for the Army Reserve and National Guard. Photo circa late 1950s or early 1960s, photographer unknown.

ticed the cute girl who lived on the corner, two houses down from where he was living, and introduced himself to her one day. My mom, Dolores Elaine Young, who was a senior in college was seven years younger than he. She was a senior in college, still dating around, and doing things that young girls do—mostly talking about boys.

Mom was born and raised in Moorestown, a small town about twelve miles outside of Philadelphia. It's a quaint town, with a lot of old money. Huge homes sit off of tree-lined streets. It was voted the best place to live by *Money* magazine in 2005.

Although the whole town is beautiful, many of the black people live on one side, and a lot of the old money, or rich, live on the other side. Today, many professional athletes live in Moorestown, such as Eagles quarterback, Donovan McNabb.

Mom was the daughter of Albert H. Young, Jr., and Anna Mae (née Myers) Young. She was the second oldest of their ten

Chester and Dolores Whittaker, my parents, as a young couple, n.d.

children: Lena (deceased), Albert (Uncle "Sonny"), Margie (deceased—her married name was Dallas), James (Uncle "Buddy"), Shirley (her married name is Watkins), Kathy, Leroy, Darlene, and Theodore were the others.

But Mom was also raised by her paternal grandparents, Albert H. Young, Sr., and Margie (née Gale) Young. Their house was a stone's throw from her parents house, and her grandparents had taken her in since her parents had so many kids.

Mom was spoiled and coddled, while many of her siblings, who lived nearby, didn't necessarily get the same attention. Since she was the oldest child living in the house at that time, she was "picked," so to speak, and she went to her grandparents. Her brother, James, Uncle "Buddy," also lived with their grandparents whom were called Nannie and Dada by the family. Family members do not remember how it was determined Uncle Buddy would live with them, too, but he did.

Mom acknowledged that moving to her grandparents' home enabled her to experience a lot of things in life that she may not have otherwise. She was sent to college, nearby Glassboro State College (now Rowan University), where she majored in education (and was an elementary school teacher for twenty-nine years). Her grandparents bought her a car. There wasn't much she didn't get in life if she wanted it, including the man of her dreams.

In April 1962 when Dad met Mom, she was sitting on the front porch of her house talking to some male friends, two or three fellows. Living two doors down at Mrs. Roy's house, he hadn't lived there that long. Dad happened to see Mom sitting out on the porch talking to other young men, and he came over and introduced himself. When he and Mom started talking, they became friends right away. The other young men left after a while. Dad was very talkative, and he introduced himself to her grandparents, too.

Mom came home from college on the weekends, and Dad and she started dating. They stayed at home quite a bit. He attended her college graduation that June.

Dolores Young, my mom, standing in the middle of her family, as she graduates from Glassboro State College. Left to right: Aunt Margaret (née Young) Hicks, Aunt Pauline Young, Mom, Nannie (Margie Young), and Grandmom (Anna Mae Young), June 1962.

Dad who was very outgoing and very honest, didn't try to hide the fact that he was separated from his wife. Mom liked his honesty. She also liked that he was just so handsome. To her he was very attractive, well-groomed, always neat. They had many things in common, except for sports. Although Dad really loved sports, she wasn't much interested in sports. She didn't know that much about football or other sports. My dad started coaching football in the fall, and Mom attended some of his games. After they started dating, he was the only one she was interested in.

As a suitor, Dad was no boy. He had finished college. He had married and been out in the world. When he and my mom met, it was as if they had known each other for a long time. With some prompting from Dad, she stopped seeing the other fellows whom she was dating.

Dad had stayed with Mrs. Roy a short time. After he found out that Anna Lucas, another neighbor, had a room to rent, he moved to her house. Mrs. Lucas lived right around the corner from Mom.

Anna Lucas took Dad in and treated him just like a son. She fell in love with the young, handsome go-getter and helped to advise him and shape and mold him into even more of a man. Because she loved him so much, she left her house to him. Although he didn't live with her very long, he made a very positive impression on her. Dad just had that way about him where people admired him. He ended up signing the house over to her nephew because he felt guilty. But the fact that she left it to him really said a lot about her opinion of him. Dad cared about her and later named one of his daughter's after her.

Mom's grandparents approved of Dad, too. They surely saw the promise in that handsome young man. They knew he would be something one day, and that he would take care of their granddaughter. Dad came to the house and ate dinner just like he was a member of the family. Nannie and Dada loved him like a son, even before he and Mom got married.

Chapter 4
Growing Family

Dad and Mom were married on August 24, 1963, in Moorestown, New Jersey, at the Second Baptist Church. They lived with Mrs. Roy for a few months. Soon able to buy their own home, Dad and Mom moved to LaGorce Square in Burlington Township, New Jersey. Their first home was a small ranch-style house with three bedrooms in a neighborhood that was heavily populated with young, up-and-coming black folk. They made friends, and they became a part of the community as the Whittakers.

Dolores and Chester Whittaker, my mom and dad, smooching on their wedding day, August 24, 1963.

Almost a week after their first anniversary, their first daughter, Michelle Yvonne, was born, on August 30, 1964, at Rancocas Valley Hospital in Willingboro, not far away. I, Celeste, their second daughter, was born on March 26, 1966, also at Rancocas Valley Hospital. Michelle's nickname was Shelly. Dad called me "Les" or "Lessie," rarely Celeste. So Chet and Dee, as they were called, had two girls, seventeen months apart. It was a growing young family.

Chester Whittaker, my dad, posing with my sister, Michelle (Shelly), and me—Celeste, at our house in Burlington Township, September 1968. Photo taken by my mom, Dolores Whittaker.

Anna Catherine was born on December 6, 1968, in Willingboro, as well. She was confident, and talkative, a lot like my dad in many ways; it was clear from the beginning that they had a special bond (so much like him, it is no surprise that at the time of this writing she is a vice president in human resources at her company.)

Dad was witty, handsome, and intelligent. A real go-getter in a world of people who sometimes don't really know what hard work means. Dad worked two jobs, like his parents. While he continued working in special education at the William R. Allen School, an elementary school for black children, he also worked cleaning a bank at night. He also made time to coach track and field at Burlington's local high school. After kissing Mom good-bye, he took a canister of hot coffee and went out the door. I don't remember him calling out or complaining that he was working two jobs; he just did it.

Dad had a college degree, but was also working toward his master's degree at Trenton State College (now The College of New Jersey). He believed because he was a young black man, he would have to have more than just the average degree to succeed.

As a coach at Burlington City High School, Dad was well-respected in Burlington County. He first was an assistant coach in football and track and was later head track coach. He was also the first cross country coach in school

Chester and Dolores Whittaker, my dad and mom holding me—Celeste, on the day Dad received his master's degree from Trenton State College, Trenton, New Jersey, September 1968.

history. When he stepped down as track coach in May of 1965 to become a demonstration teacher at Trenton State College, several of the local papers published articles about him.

"I am happy about my new position, but sorry to leave the Burlington School system," Dad told the *Burlington County Times* (May 22, 1965). "I had a great opportunity as head coach and enjoyed working with the boys. It was a tough decision to make. This is a once in a lifetime opportunity and I couldn't pass it by. My family comes first and I know this is a step in the right direction."

My dad was so handsome, so alive, and so much fun. When my mom was not at home, Dad took care of us. On one particular night when I was three-years-old, I remembered Dad taking care of Michelle, Anna, who was two years younger than me and still a baby, and me. He played music for us, the Beatles, Otis Redding, and the Supremes, on a stereo that was inside of a wooden cabinet. We sang the songs and danced around the house. Dad sang harder—in that booming voice—than we girls sang. Then, he made us ice cream floats, and I ate some Oreo cookies, my favorites at the time. What a fun, fun night. There would be many more of those times.

I don't want to act like my house was perfect. We had some things come against us as a family, but we worked through it as a family. Growing up in

Chester and Dolores Whittaker, my dad and mom, had four daughters. Left to right: Anna, me—Celeste, Michelle (Shelly), and Monica dancing at our house in Illinois in June 1972.

a household which put God first meant something. We were a praying family, so when roadblocks, bumps, challenges, or trials came up, the Lord really kept us and helped get us through them.

Dad and Mom did the best they could by us, and they made us feel like we were somebody. That's the greatest gift you can give a child: to make them feel special. To make them feel as if what they are saying has merit and is important. It helps them with their self-esteem and gives them confidence.

Chapter 5
Job in the Midwest

After living in that house in Burlington for a few years, Dad, being the aggressive man that he was, looked for bigger and better things. Dad applied for a job with the National School Boards Association near Chicago, Illinois, and, not surprisingly, he got it, becoming the organization's director of minority affairs. It was something he wanted to do. He wanted to work for the National School Boards Association because holding a national position was prestigious.

Dad and Mom sold the house, a decision my mom later said was a mistake, and moved the family to the Chicago suburbs. It was cold, cold, cold. They really thought the family would stay out there, but it just didn't work out. They were only in Illinois for two years.

For Mom the move was difficult, and she can't say that she really wanted to move out there. She had started teaching in Willingboro, New Jersey, and after they moved to Burlington, she worked for Burlington City, then Burlington Township. She was very attached to their house in LaGorce. She loved LaGorce Square and they had so many friends that she hated to leave. She believed that they were really sorry we sold the house. After moving to Illinois, she didn't work at all. She was a stay-at-home mom, which was unusual for her. But having four kids contributed to her staying at home.

We first lived in Northfield, Illinois, in a townhouse with a full basement. It was where I first learned to ride a bike. The memory is so clear. On the day my dad took the training wheels off my bike, he stood there and told me to ride. I looked back, frightened, but he looked calm and confident and was smiling. Whew, I knew everything was going to be just fine.

I rode and rode some more. I had stopped using training wheels, and Dad stood there with his arms crossed, looking proudly at me ride. I didn't fall off that day. When I think back, that day was symbolic, for the rest of my life, really. Dad gave me my wings to fly that day, and he would continue to do that so many more times over the years.

In that same townhouse in Northfield, we had a major addition to our family, my baby sister Monica. The day of her birth was both exciting and scary. I was in my room, and I heard my mom hustling to the bathroom. There was water all over the floor, and I heard my mom say, "My water broke." My dad rushed her to the hospital, and Monica Leigh Whittaker was born on February 12, 1971, in Evanston, Illinois. I remember we almost named her Nicole, but Monica won out. Now Dad and Mom had four girls, Michelle, me, Anna, and Monica. As mentioned before, we also had an older sister Saundra, whom Dad had from a previous marriage.

The hospital talked of giving Monica a blood transfusion because she was so pale. Dad told those doctors off and told them to look at him. He was a very light-skinned black man, after all. Why did it seem so odd that his baby would be fair? There was no answer. He'd won that debate.

I remember listening to tapes of Rev. Dr. Martin Luther King, Jr., when we lived in Illinois. Dad later taped my sisters and me reciting the speeches, or as I call it, "doing our thing." On one occasion, I was repeating a part of King's famous, "I have a dream" speech, Shelly was singing, and Anna kept saying, "I two and a half, daddy, I two and a half.'" I repeat that story not because there's anything earth shattering there. But just imagine we were three little girls who were comfortable enough with their mom and their dad to recite speeches, sing, just doing their thing with no embarrassment or fear that someone would say, "shut up and sit down." It was a wonderful, wonderful thing. Dad and Mom encouraged us to express ourselves and gave us confidence. This happened at our second home in Illinois.

Chester Whittaker, my dad, who is partially visible on the right side of the picture, eating breakfast with his girls. Starting clockwise, with me—Celeste, my back to the camera, Michelle (Shelly), Monica, and Anna in 1972.

Chapter 6
Back in New Jersey

Settling in Willingboro

We returned to New Jersey after two years; that's where most of my mom's family lived. Since we had sold our house in Burlington Township, we ended up in Willingboro, a commuter's town where many of the working adults either worked in Philadelphia, thirty minutes away, or in New York, about ninety minutes away.

First we lived at 6 Holstone Lane. Later, we moved to 73 Hillcrest Lane, and what a time we had there. Our house soon became the neighborhood hangout. There were four of us girls, and the boys noticed. We were all just friendly and enjoyed having a good time. The bench in front of our house always seemed to have plenty of people sitting on it. We played kickball out in the street or touch football or tag. Later on, we played basketball which became my favorite sport to my dad's great delight.

Dad who absolutely loved sports taught me about football when I was younger, explaining the rules of the game. We used to sit and watch the Eagles sometimes on Sundays, but he absolutely loved the Philadelphia 76ers basketball team. So did I.

He took me to my first Sixers game when I was about eleven or twelve. That's back when Dr. J., George McInnis, Doug Collins, and Darryl Dawkins were on the team. I loved it instantly and became a lifelong fan, which is ironic, because as I said, I later covered the Sixers as a sportswriter for the *Courier-Post*.

Coaching a daughter in basketball

I was in class at Hawthorne Park Elementary School in Willingboro, when someone passed a flyer around that said the Police Athletic League was forming a youth girls basketball league. I was a big fan of Julius "Dr. J" Erving who was playing for the NBA's Philadelphia 76ers at that time. I wanted to make my best impression of Erving, so I tried out.

Not only did I make the team, but being one of the tallest girls out there, I managed to win the most valuable player trophy that year, leading the league in scoring. My dad and my mom were at all of my games, with my dad screaming "come on Celeste." I remember him at our awards ceremony beaming proudly as his twelve-year-old tomboy went up to collect her very first trophy. It was one of the proudest moments of my life, made that much sweeter with Daddy looking on. There would be many more of those moments over the years as I continued to play basketball through high school and get better and better.

It would have never happened had I not had that basketball goal in my backyard that my dad and my mom purchased for me when they learned that I wanted to play. My dad and I would go out there and shoot or I would go out there by myself and just practice on my own or the kids from the neighborhood and I used to play countless games of HORSE or one-on-one.

The funny thing is, I know Dad enjoyed coaching, but I think he enjoyed "coaching" me most of all. Those backyard lessons and encouragement at my games are something I have never forgotten.

That's something that I will always remember, because those backyard games with my dad and the kids weren't just about getting better at basketball. They were about learning discipline and learning that if you wanted to be really good at something—whether it's basketball, drawing, dancing, singing, swimming, cooking—whatever, you have to do it over and over again and perfect your craft.

Nothing comes easy in life. The best are the best for a reason. Sure, God-given ability counts for something, but Michael Jordan or Tiger Woods didn't get to be at their level without hours and hours of practice and working on their skills.

That's what I learned. I improved in those backyard sessions and by going away to basketball camps. And, later on, I played at the local basketball courts with the guys.

So, when I earned that most valuable player award after my first season of playing PAL, it was one of my proudest moments in my

Celeste Whittaker, the author, as a basketball player for Willingboro High School, warming up before a game at Lenape High School in Medford, N.J., 1983.

life to that point. I could see where my hard work had paid off, and I could see where my dad's encouragement had paid off.

I attended Willingboro High School in South Jersey. Ironically, one of my old PAL coaches was already a star on the basketball team. Her name was Kim Butler. Meanwhile, I was still going to the courts and playing with guys and shooting for hours in my yard.

I remember Dad driving us to school in the morning. He used to say to me, "You're going to be a basketball star." It's like he fed that to me all the time, and I really believed it, and I did become that. He saw to it. I became an all-star basketball player at Willingboro High School and earned a full athletic scholarship to the University of North Carolina at Chapel Hill (Dad called them and sent them a tape of me, and that's how they learned about me). My mom and my dad came to every one of my high school games.

What that illustrates is not only the power of words, but the power of a parents' words. In the same way you can feed your children positive, you can feed them negative thoughts, too. That means telling them they're ugly, too short, too dumb, never going to be anything. Those words sting, and have a long-lasting effect. Why not try telling them that they're smart, beautiful, talented or that they can do or be anything that they want in life?

Celeste Whittaker, the author, as a basketball player at University of North Carolina, Chapel Hill, in 1984. UNC Athletic Department photo.

Chapter 7
Oh, Brother

Because Dad fell in love with New Jersey while stationed at Fort Dix, he was also responsible for his brother relocating here. While teaching at the William R. Allen School in Burlington, he convinced Uncle Clarence to move to New Jersey to take up a vacant teaching position there with him. At that time his brother was about to become a New York City police officer, but Dad convinced him to come to New Jersey.

Uncle Clarence stayed with Mom's family in Moorestown while getting situated. Dad who was such a mover and a shaker motivated his brother to work in the field of education. He followed Dad to at least four of his other jobs. Some of the places they worked together were the William R. Allen School (Burlington City), William L. Antheil Elementary School (Ewing Township), Edward R. Johnstone Training and Research Center (Bordentown, was the Manual Training and Industrial School for Colored Youth until 1955), Trenton State College demonstration faculty, and Burlington County College (BCC). Dad started the first Educational Opportunity Fund Program at BCC, which Uncle Clarence later directed. Daddy also served as the assistant to the president for the college's first president, N. Dean Evans.

Chester Whittaker, my dad, and Clarence Whittaker, my uncle, at Uncle Clarence's house in Tabernacle, New Jersey, circa 1992.

That is how the Jersey connection all began, and the Whittaker children were born and raised in South Jersey. Dad and Uncle Clarence, both handsome men who wore glasses, were hard working, intelligent, family men who loved their wives and children greatly.

Uncle Clarence and Aunt Liz (Elizabeth (née Smith) Whittaker) had five daughters, Lisa, Gina, Clare, Pam and Karla, and a son, Clarence Jr. Three of the siblings, Gina, Pam, and Clarence, became lawyers, and Pam married one of the top lawyers in the country, Milton Marquis. My cousins all grew up in Pemberton and graduated from Pemberton High School, about a half hour away from Willingboro. My sisters and I all graduated from Willingboro High School.

Anna told me about a time when Uncle Clarence was knocking on our front door at our house at 65 Courtland Lane in Willingboro, New Jersey, and Dad went running and hid in the laundry room of the house. Someone let Uncle in, and he walked back to the den, which was right near the laundry room. My dad jumped out, trying to "scare" my uncle. My dad's family called him "Junior" and he and my uncle often referred to each other as boy. "Hey boy, how you doing boy?"

Whittaker family members share Thanksgiving Day, in Willingboro, New Jersey, November 1981. Seated, left to right: Clarence, Sr., my uncle, partly visible, Liz, my aunt—Uncle Clarence's wife, and Gina, my cousin— Uncle Clarence's and Aunt Liz's daughter. Left to right, standing: Dolores, my mom, Chester, my dad.

Clarence Jr., or "Little Clarence," as we've called him over the years, is my age; we both graduated from high school in 1984. The rest of us are all pretty close in age. I remember once, Karla and I actually played a basketball game against each other in high school. I think she was a senior, and I was a sophomore. We battled mightily. She teased me later on, saying that I had elbowed her and basically acted like I didn't really know her on the court. Well, we both played each other rough. We weren't cousins when we were playing, but we hugged and talked afterwards.

Our families were out in the crowd watching the game, and looking back, that was a unique experience that never happened for me again in high school.

We loved all of our cousins on both sides of our family, but I guess it was extra special with my dad and his brother because it was only the two of them. There weren't any other siblings. We grew up and were very close to our cousins, with both sides making regular visits over the years.

Going out to Uncle Clarence's house in Pemberton was always fun. It was like an adventure. There was always a house full, and we'd laugh and talk and joke with our cousins, while the grown-ups chatted upstairs.

The Whittakers in Tabernacle, New Jersey., circa 1992. Front, l. to r.: Clarence, Sr., my uncle, Pam Marquis Whittaker and Clare Whittaker (my cousins), Dolores, my mom. Seated on couch, l. to r.: my cousin Clarence Jr., me—Celeste, my cousin Gina, my sister Michelle (Shelly) Adderley, baby Ashley Adderley, my niece. Standing, left to right: Chester, my dad, Liz, my aunt.

I remember that one of the best times I ever had on New Year's Eve was with my cousins. Mr. and Mrs. Clarence Martin had two sons, Doug and Michael. They were having a party in their Burlington Township home. They were a little older than me. I was still in high school, but my parents let me go because my cousins came to pick me up. Boy, did we have a ball. Mr. Martin is deceased now, unfortunately. But, we were at their house with food and great music until the wee hours of the morning.

We danced, fast and slow, and just had a wonderful time. We laughed and talked and partied. I don't think I got in until after 2 a.m., but again, I was safe and sound with my cousins and my family was fine with that. Daddy knew I was with "Brother's" kids, so he knew I'd be just fine.

Clarence Whittaker, my uncle, Anna (née Whittaker) Mitchell, my sister, and me— Celeste Whittaker, at Uncle Clarence's home in Tabernacle, New Jersey, November 1998.

Chapter 8
Newport News and the Farm

Vacationing in Newport News, Virginia

When my dad was growing up in Newport News, many in the community held jobs at the Newport News shipyard, including his father, Chester Whitaker, as I stated earlier. Granddaddy also worked for the U.S. Post Office as a mechanic and retired from the post office after many years of service. The trades of the community today include shipbuilding, technological research, and international commerce. Newport News had its negative points, as an urban area with housing projects like any other city. In fact, my dad didn't grow up that far away from that.

The Whittakers visit Newport News, Virginia for Easter. Front, l. to r.: Anna, Michelle (Shelly), Monica, and me—Celeste. Back, l. to r.: Chester Whittaker, my dad, Hazel Whitaker—Nana, and Chester Whitaker—Granddaddy, n.d.

We used to vacation in Newport News every summer, spending a week or so with my Dad's parents. We'd sit out on the porch on 1033 East. 32nd Street or we'd walk up to my dad's old high school and go to the track. We'd eat some wonderful meals prepared by my grandmother; we called her Nana and she could cook anything and make it excellent. Or we would visit relatives who lived nearby, such as Uncle Royster Whitaker or Aunt Sister (Florence Brown), or my dad's friend, Claude Carter, whom he had known since his days at Virginia State.

Even though as kids it wasn't the most exciting way to spend a week, we learned about our family history. Mainly we got to spend some time with our grandparents who we didn't get to see often.

I remember sitting out back in a covered picnic area and eating watermelon with my sisters, sitting in the den area my granddad had built with his bare hands, or sleeping upstairs, the same upstairs my granddad had built, in one of the two bedrooms, which were spacious and so neat.

Sometimes my sisters and I worked on some type of art project. We were into painting one year and another year we did hook rugs. We'd work on it for the week we were down there, then would leave a parting little trinket for our grandparents. Years later, they still had a few of the paintings we did and the hook rugs, too.

Chester Whittaker, my dad, with his parents, Chester Whitaker—Granddaddy, and Hazel Whitaker—Nana, in Willingboro, N.J., circa 1995.

My father was very happy when we visited his parents. He was in his element. He and his brother called their parents Momma and Daddy, and he always seemed to fall back into his Southern accent whenever he talked to them or his brother on the phone or in person. Mom thought they were wonderful and such down to earth people. She met them the year before Dad and she got married, and they treated her almost like a daughter-in-law already.

Dad was more like his father than his mom. His dad was very open, very talkative, very outgoing, while his mom was conservative and laid-back. His dad had that personality where you couldn't help but love him. His mom was special, too. In the two of them, you could see that they were just a very loving family.

It's funny. Dad was a country boy at heart and he liked nothing more than to be around his family. We didn't get to get down there nearly as much as he would have liked to, but we got down there enough.

One of his mother's brothers, Uncle Dock Kearney, lived in Glen Burnie, Maryland, and we would visit his farm many summers, as well. My dad actually favored Uncle Dock some. We would go to the farm and spend a week or so. They had chickens and pigs. It was a real farm. Aunt Annabelle, Uncle Dock's wife, used to use the eggs right from those chickens to cook us breakfast.

Hazel Whitaker—Nana, my dad's mother, and Chester Whittaker, my dad, in Newport News, Virginia. Dad bought her the suit that she was wearing in this photo.

There wasn't a whole lot to do there, so we'd play down on the farm or go shoot hoops. One of their sons, Earl, and his two sons, Gary and Earl Jr., also lived on part of their property, so we'd spend time with the boys who were close to our age.

As much as my sisters and I thought we were kind of cool, there was something really educational and eye-opening about spending time on a farm for a week or so. You saw how other people lived and what their daily experiences were like compared to yours.

You saw that there were different ways of getting things done on a day-to-day basis and that you could be self-sufficient in a way. You could raise your own chickens, pigs and the like. You could actually eat food provided by the animals that you were raising. Self-sufficient in that sense as opposed to being totally reliant on the local grocery store.

It also taught me about family. The fact that they opened their home to us—and there were six of us—for a week says something. They wouldn't think of us staying at a hotel, and they certainly never told my dad we couldn't come.

There was always plenty of food, and other relatives would come around. Uncle Lewis Kearney, Nana and Uncle Dock's brother, lived in nearby Baltimore, Maryland, where he owned a barbershop, so he would come around sometimes.

I remember one time, Uncle Dock let us drive his tractor. We were sort of playing on it, but it got stuck up on a hilly area near the house. The tractor was about to tip over, and my dad came running out of the house, and got in between the tractor and the cart with kids in it that it was pulling.

Dad suffered a very deep cut on his leg as he wrestled with the gears on the tractor and got us out of any danger. I felt so bad because I had been driving the tractor and his leg got caught. I was so scared because I thought his leg might get cut off or have to be amputated later. He was okay, other than the cut, which looked really bad at the time. It actually healed up quite nicely, and thankfully, did not get infected.

But I remember thinking how brave my dad was. I know it was only a tractor, but he didn't think twice before running out there and getting us out of any kind of danger.

Chapter 9
Taking Celeste to College

I remember the day so clearly. I had indeed earned a full basketball scholarship to the University of North Carolina at Chapel Hill. My family and I were headed to Chapel Hill to drop me off at school. Dad loaded up the car — and I do mean loaded it up— and I and my two younger sisters, my mom and my dad were off to North Carolina. I think my sister, Shelly, was working, so she didn't go.

Of course, we had to make a few pit stops. We drove the white Lincoln down I-95. We ended up stopping in Petersburg, Virginia, to visit J. B. Sanders so my dad could get measured for a suit. In the meantime, we played with the dog, had a meal, and they had grown up talk and talked some more.

Meanwhile, I was an anxious eighteen-year-old who couldn't wait to get to school. I couldn't believe my trip to college had turned into some social visit with my dad's friend. I was a little irritated to say the least. All I could think about was Chapel Hill. I wanted to see my dorm, meet new friends, and start my new life. But we visited some more, and some more.

See, that was my dad. He was a social butterfly, if there ever was one. We used to have huge cookouts at our house in the summers. I remember other big parties as well. Once, our grandparents even had a re-commitment ceremony, with a preacher and all, at our house. My sister Shelly had her wedding at our house. I don't know how we fit all those chairs into our living room, but we had an organist, a soloist, and a wonderful catered affair. My dad loved to entertain, he just enjoyed people. He was always considerate of Mom. She had affairs catered, and she would get trays of prepared foods.

Whittaker family and guests at Michelle (Shelly's) wedding, December 19, 1987. Front row only, l. to r.: Nannie (Margie Young), Aunt Margaret Hicks, Sara Adderley, Dolores and Chester Whittaker, my mom and dad.

Well, back to my college story. Finally, we said our good-byes and headed down I-85. We finally pulled into Chapel Hill around 10 p.m. that night. We had left about 7:30 that morning. Keep in mind, it's usually about a seven hour ride (I later learned). We stayed at the Chapel Hill Inn, a quaint little hotel on the UNC campus. The next morning, I was over at my dorm so I could check in.

My dad pulled the Lincoln up in front of Morrison Hall in the circle. I got out, surveyed the land, and decided I kind of liked the brick multi-storied building: This was my new home.

Dad was excitedly looking for my college teammate—Kathy Wilson— who we heard would be living on the same floor as me right across the hall. When a tall girl walked by, Dad kept saying, "That might be Kathy."

Actually, he was responsible for me going to school at Carolina. He had written the coach, Jennifer Alley, about me and I believe he sent them a tape of me playing basketball. They soon recruited me. With dad being a North Carolina native, he was so excited that the Tar Heels were interested in having me. When it was time for me to go on my recruiting visit my senior year, he went with me.

The Whittakers, my family, move me—Celeste, to college. Front, l. to r.: my dad, Chester, my sister Monica. Back, l. to r.: me, my sister Anna, my mom, Dolores, in my dorm room in Morrison Hall, University of North Carolina, Chapel Hill, August 1984.

So, it was no surprise that on *that* summer day in 1984 he was the most excited of us all. My mom and sisters were fairly quiet, as was I. I figured, I'd meet Kathy soon enough. About an hour later, I saw the tall, skinny girl with the jheri curl across the hall from me. She was just as calm as I was, dancing, twisting her neck around, doing this dance I later learned was called "The Prep."

Her mother, Vivian, was busily preparing her room, as my folks were doing for me. Her dad, Joe, was there as well. My dad introduced himself, and we all introduced ourselves. Little did I know that Kathy and I would become lifelong friends. We started off as teammates, quickly became roommates, and are great friends to this day, some twenty-three years later. Her parents are like second parents to me. A few years after I graduated from college, they allowed me to live with them in Atlanta for a year, when I moved there after working in New York City at *Business Week* magazine for two years. They treated me like I was actually their daughter, and I've never forgotten that.

That day at Carolina, my parents stayed, helped me get set up, bought me some groceries and then when it was time for them to return to New Jersey, they dropped me off on a different part of campus, near the student bookstore. I remember thinking, "this is it," as they pulled off in the Lincoln, headed back to New Jersey. I didn't look back at the car. I didn't want to burst out crying.

This was the start of my new life. I was so much a daddy and mommy's girl, that I wanted to run after the car, crying. But I didn't. I turned and walked towards the bookstore. I realized, I was all alone. It was a scary feeling, but just for a minute. I smiled and walked into the student bookstore. I never did cry.

I went through a trial as a freshman in college, and it was then that I really wished my parents were nearby. I had never been really injured since I started playing basketball, but I wasn't completely prepared for the rigorous training we would go through on the basketball team. We had a track program, that's right. We had to run a mile in under seven minutes, and we had to run about twelve 220-yard sprints around the track under a certain time. The days we weren't running, we lifted weights. This was in the pre-season.

My legs were extremely achy after the first few days, but I pushed through. The track program was the toughest part of it all. There were many days I didn't think I would make it through, but Kat encouraged me and pushed me.

Once practice started, I felt a twinge in my left leg. I believed I had pulled a hamstring muscle. I sat out of practice for several days. Not long after my return, we were doing a press break drill. I turned to catch a pass and came down, twisting my knee. I heard a "snap." I went down in a heap and was in terrible pain. Our trainer, Clairbeth Lehn, came rushing over, looked at my knee, and it seemed to be pretty serious. I would later find out that I had torn the anterior cruciate ligament in the knee. I hadn't even made it to the first game, and I was already out for the year!

Needless to say that I was devastated. I called home, crying. My mom and my dad offered me comfort, but there was really nothing they could do. I later ended up having to have arthroscopic surgery on the knee. I had torn cartilage as well. They repaired the cartilage, but Dr. Timothy Taft, one of the top orthopedic surgeons in the country, recommended that I not get the major surgery done to repair the ligament. That would've required a six inch incision in my knee, which would've left a bad scar on the knee. Since there weren't many options for women to play basketball after college back then, I had three or four more years left to play at the most, more than likely. He recommended that I rehab the knee, get it stronger than the other one, and perhaps wear a brace. That's what I did.

Even though I wasn't playing, my dad still came down to North Carolina when we played in the Atlantic Coast Conference Tournament that spring. The tournament was in Fayetteville, North Carolina. We had a cousin there, so Dad made a weekend of it.

Chester Whittaker, my dad, and me—Celeste Whittaker, the author, at Carmichael Auditorium, University of North Carolina, Chapel Hill, March 1985.

He came down from New Jersey, he even stayed in our team hotel. I was a little embarrassed, but now looking back, I should have been flattered.

Kathy's mom and her friend Mrs. Doris Anderson were also there. Mrs. Anderson was light-skinned, my dad quickly began to call her "Big Red." Dad hung out with them and had a wonderful time. He was a life of the party kind of person. Years later, Mrs. Anderson often asked me how my dad was.

When I returned home for the summer, Dad set me up at a rehab facility in Marlton, New Jersey. I went there daily and did weight work and other things to get my knee stronger. I also began to run around the track, preparing for the rigorous track season. The knee did get back to full strength and after I returned to Carolina that summer, I played pickup games again and felt fine.

I made it through the pre-season conditioning, the dreaded track program, and even made it to the first game of the season. We played Maryland Eastern Shore at home and won 102-54. I got in for a few minutes, and I was so excited. Our next trip was Florida. We visited Disney World while down there and I had great time. However, at practice one day, ironically, the same girl who had thrown me the same pass on the same press break drill when I was initially injured, threw it again. I went down in a heap again. I heard a pop again. I knew what that meant.

This time I decided I didn't necessarily want to try to come back to play

again. I went through the rehab and I got the knee strong again. But I did not play that season. I decided in the spring that I would get a medical release. That meant I would still have my education paid for, but the team could use my scholarship to sign another player.

Celeste Whittaker, the author, as a member of the basketball team at University of North Carolina, Chapel Hill. UNC Athletic Department photo, fall 1985.

Regretfully, I made the decision before actually talking to my dad. I did that, because I knew he would try to talk me out of it. I wrote him a very long detailed letter, explaining my position and explaining that I wanted to focus on being a student now. I could tell he was hurt that I had not discussed it all with him first, but I thought he was also okay with the fact that I had thought it out for myself, weighed the pros and cons as he had always taught me, and made my final decision.

I never played in another game at Carolina, but my dad remained as proud of me as he had always been. The whole family came down when I graduated in May of 1988 with a B.A. in journalism, and it was an extremely proud moment for me.

There was a funny moment that happened after graduation that kind of sums Dad up, too. I had an interview at *Business Week* magazine in New York City. I had never driven to New York by myself, so my dad volunteered to take me.

Chester Whittaker, my dad, shakes the hand of a security guard at Kenan Stadium, University of North Carolina, Chapel Hill, on my graduation day in May 1988.

We drove up to Manhattan from South Jersey one weekday afternoon. We arrived at West 49th Street and 6th Avenue at the McGraw Hill building, right across from the famous Radio City Music Hall, where the interview was located.

It was near lunch time, so I told Dad he could hang out near the building, grab something to eat, and relax. I also told him I would be down soon. He agreed.

Well, the interview lasted nearly two hours. I did pretty well and they had several people talk to me. When one of the executive assistants to the editor of the magazine was interviewing me, out of the corner of my eye, I saw my dad coming towards me down the hallway.

I was flabbergasted. He had gotten through the security area and had talked his way into the magazine's 50th floor office as well. You had to actually be buzzed in by the receptionist to get back into the offices.

I shooed him away with my hand, and he started backing down the hallway and went back out the door. It's something that I laugh about now, but back then, I confronted him about it and he said the interview had taken so long, he figured he'd come to see what was going on.

That was Dad!!!

Chapter 10
Dad the Pioneer

Education and government service

Chester M. Whittaker understood the value of education. Not only did he graduate from Virginia State College, (now Virginia State University) with a B.S. degree in recreational therapy, but he later obtained a masters degree from Trenton State College (now The College of New Jersey) in special education and completed requirements for principal, supervisor, and chief school administrator certificates at Rider College (now Rider University).

As discussed in chapter 3, one of his early jobs was at the William R. Allen School in Burlington, New Jersey, where he taught for five years. He also served with the New Jersey Department of Education, as a supervisor in the New Jersey Correctional Program. Uncle Clarence confirmed that my dad was never afraid to take risks, and this quality helped him obtain positions that were rare at that time for black people. His impressive, deep,

Chester Whittaker, my dad, always dressed very professionally, whether teaching or carrying out his work for federal and New Jersey state agencies.

and booming voice translated into confidence to those around him. He also did not hesitate to move or to work out of state when necessary.

Dad's primary responsibilities with the correctional program at that time were working with reformatories that trained young or first offenders in New Jersey, such as the Annandale Reformatory For Boys (now the Mountainview Youth Correctional Facility), the Bordentown Reformatory (now called the Youth Correctional Facility at Bordentown), the New Jersey State Home for Boys near Jamesburg (originally the New Jersey State Reform School, later the Training School for Boys, and now the New Jersey Training School for Boys), and the Clinton State Home for Girls. He would often speak at the institutions, and he said that he would often tell the boys and girls that it was not "Black power" that they needed, but "brain power" instead.

In an interview with the *Burlington County Times* (October 24, 1968), my dad said this about his work with the young people:

> It wasn't easy. My heart went out to those boys and girls. There they were, just youngsters, really, and they had two strikes against them already. My job was to show them that a Negro COULD make it if he worked hard enough. I spoke before many of these institutions and I didn't hand them any platitudes or ready made optimistic phrases. You can't fool young people that way. I told them how it really is on the outside. I told them that the opportunities were there if they worked hard. And the fact that I'm black myself was proof of that. We could communicate. They could see and identify.
>
> Of course, many of them could not be reached, but then again, many could. You'd be surprised at the number of young men and women in these reformatories who are continuing their education. Some of them are working very hard despite the very great handicaps. That's why I feel bad when I see those boys and girls on the outside who don't have such handicaps, wasting their precious opportunities.

After leaving this position, he became assistant to the president at Burlington County College where he founded a program to give financial aid to students, particularly minorities.

For two years (that's why we moved to Illinois), he was the director of minority affairs for the National School Boards Association in Illinois. Later, after returning to New Jersey, Dad was a special assistant to former governor Brendan Byrne. In that role, he was the principal advisor to the governor on such matters as human service planning and minority problems. He once helped Pilgrim Baptist Church in Newark obtain a $450,000 grant from the state for an urban revitalization plan. Dad was the only black serving on the governor's staff in a policy making position. During the time he worked for the governor, he was on leave from the federal service (U.S. Department of Health Education and Welfare) at the request of the governor's office. Dad had been a federal employee, serving at the executive level for a ten-year period.

Dad was also president of the Association for Schools and Agencies for the Handicapped (ASAH), which comprises seventy-eight approved private schools throughout New Jersey. He was the first minority to serve in that capacity. That organization honored him after his death as Humanitarian of the Year in 1997.

His last job was as the executive director for Archway Programs where he was responsible for approximately 350 students and staff. He was the principal spokesperson for the agency in all program related matters.

Reverend Art Lewis, a former director of the Office of Economic Opportunity, New Jersey Department of Community Affairs, knew Dad for many years. He remembered Dad's deep laugh and the fact that Dad was always one step ahead. Reverend Lewis considered my dad as a visionary, and confirmed that Dad didn't take no for an answer when trying to accomplish things, and that Uncle Clarence was also accomplished.

Tom Kean, governor of New Jersey, stands at the podium while reading a proclamation, as Chester Whittaker, my dad who is standing far right, looks on, in 1984.

Chester Whittaker, my dad, joins other officials at a ribbon-cutting ceremony where he later spoke, n.d.

Awards for excellence and service

Dad won numerous awards in his life, including the Club Blue Chip Achievement Award in 1978, the Four Chaplains Humanitarian Award in 1970, and in 1979, Second Baptist Church awarded him the Martin Luther King Jr. Award for his efforts in emulating the life of Dr. King in the church and in the community.

One of his proudest honors was being named Father of the Year in 1989 by Second Baptist Church. He was also very proud that in 1966, when he served as an outstanding demonstration teacher at Trenton State College, that he won an all-expense paid trip to Canada for the Council on Exceptional Children's Convention.

He believed in hard work. I don't ever remember him being unemployed. I also don't remember him every laying up in the bed sick or calling out of work. That just wasn't Dad. Nor do I ever remember us wanting for anything growing up.

Mom confirmed that Dad was always thinking of extra ways to make money. The examples were when he cleaned up at a bank in Mount Holly at night, worked as a security guard at a hospital, and worked at The Children's Home. After he retired from Archway, he taught a course at Camden County College, he also did educational consulting at a private school in Vineland, New Jersey.

Above: Chester Whittaker, my dad, hugs Clarence Whittaker Sr., his brother and my uncle, after Dad received the Reverend Martin Luther King Jr. award from Second Baptist Church, in Moorestown, New Jersey, for his efforts in emulating the life of the late leader, December 1979. Below: Dad shakes hands with Fate Kearney, his maternal uncle, at the same awards ceremony at Second Baptist Church in 1979.

Dad never stayed still, he always kept busy. He never wanted his family to want for anything. Whenever he was assigned to a task, he wanted to be the best that he could at whatever he did. He was very devoted and committed. If he was assigned to do something, he really did what he was supposed to do. When he was a trustee at Second Baptist Church or a deacon at St. John Baptist Church, he was always there, always did his part. He also served on the board of trustees at Richard Stockton State College of New Jersey, faithfully making the hour-long drive to Pomona to attend the monthly meetings.

His calling, I believe, was helping people in general. He had a special way with people. But his specific area was special education, and he was great in that.

Right: Chester Whittaker, my dad, received the Father of the Year Award from Reverend Casey Kimbrough at Second Baptist Church, Moorestown, New Jersey, June 1989. Below: Chester Whittaker delivers a commencement address at the Richard Stockton State College, commonly called Stockton State, circa 1996 or 1997.

Chapter 11
A Helping Hand

Mr. Westry Horne and my dad met when they worked for the Department of Health, Education and Welfare in New York City's World Trade Center. The twin towers were, of course, later destroyed in the 9-11 terrorist attacks in 2001. Mr. Horne was a supervisor at HEW. He told me that he and my dad often talked about a concept that they called the multiplication of power.

Dad defined the concept as a way to help other black people advance in their careers. When a black person moved into a position of authority, he or she could recruit other qualified blacks to fill openings when they came up. That did not mean hiring a black person just for the sake of hiring a black person, but finding a qualified candidate who is also black. If the person was not in the position to hire the recruit, he or she could bring the recruit to the attention of the person who was able to hire them. He felt it was important to increase the number of minorities at his place of employment but, again, by always making sure that the candidate was a solid candidate.

Reverend Art Lewis who knew Dad and Mr. Horne for many years and still misses his talks with them confirmed that is what they did. He did the same; anytime he had a job in state government, or whatever, he looked for college graduates to help their careers. My dad would call him to tell him about a position and to ask his opinion about which people could do the work. Dad did not want a black person to miss having the opportunity to get a job because they were not recruited for the position. Dad believed in racial and gender equality, and he was instrumental in bringing many women and minorities into the professional world of work, as attested to by Uncle Clarence.

Dad and Mr. Horne helped people get jobs at the U.S. Department of Health Education and Welfare (HEW, now the U.S. Department of Health & Human Services (HHS)), and they became fast friends, despite a twenty-year age gap. They were like-minded individuals, Christian men, with southern roots who loved their families and enjoyed good, solid friendships. They were both very accomplished men, who happened to be Alpha men as well.

When I graduated from college and was offered a job at *Business Week* magazine in New York, my parents were trying to help me figure out where I was going to live. New York was about a one and a half hours commute from Willingboro, which was a little far. We thought about a cousin that lived in

Jamaica, Queens, but I didn't know her very well, plus she had her grown son living there, and I didn't know if I'd be comfortable. Enter Dad. He remembered that Mr. Horne and his wife, Dorothy, lived in Plainfield, which was in North Jersey, and he knew they had an empty house. Both of their daughters, Judi and Jackie, were grown and living in their own homes, but they visited often.

Dad called Mr. Horne and asked if it'd be okay for me to stay with them. There was no hesitation. I was more than welcome to come. They had an apartment upstairs, with its own bathroom. I could stay there as long as I wanted to.

So, my whole family, plus my friend, Sharon Byrd, helped me move into my new digs. I was a little antsy, though. While I knew the Hornes were good people, I was twenty-two-years-old and fresh out of college. I wondered about having freedom. I didn't want to play my music too loud or be a bother to them in anyway, but I also wanted to feel at home. None of that would be an issue.

What a beautiful couple they were. They were both retired, but were still extremely active in the community as well as with their church and fraternities and sororities. They had meetings all week long. They were also still both asked to speak at various functions. Mrs. Horne was known for her performances as Mary McLeod Bethune. She had known her personally and would put on shows, acting as if she were Ms. Bethune, telling the history of this great woman. Both were gifted speakers.

The thing was, there was real, tangible love in that home. Mr. Horne was so spoiled. Mrs. Horne would cook his meals and put them on a tray, so he could sit in his chair and eat. I remember once she was going away for a week and she made sure his meals were in ready to heat up trays and only had to be put in the oven for a few minutes.

We'd eat at the dining room table every night. She was a wonderful cook and fixed some of the best meals, all kinds of chicken, fish and turkey. Home made soups. Cabbage. And her famous homemade rolls, and three Ps jam. They were known throughout Plainfield.

On Saturday's, I remember her fried apples, eggs, bacon, and rolls. I once told Mrs. Horne, a retired home economics teacher, that I was seldom sick when I lived there. I had so many fresh vegetables and homemade soups, it was nearly impossible.

I remember many evenings, being anxious to actually get home. I enjoyed talking to them in the evenings. It was like a history lesson at times, plus they had such a great relationship. I remember she used to call him "Sweetening Bug" and he'd laugh and say, "That's not my given name. That's not what my momma named me." He'd look at me and say, "Celeste, don't follow behind her and call a man Sweetening Bug. You'll never end up marrying." I told him it didn't look like he was going anywhere.

We had a lot of fun. I was made to feel like a part of the family for sure. Their daughters and granddaughter Monica all accepted me like I was a member of the family. I remember when I was considering the move to Atlanta, Judi sat me down for hours and gave me a good old-fashioned pep talk, which helped me get on my way. That's what kind of people they were!

Unfortunately, Mr. Horne died about four years after I returned to New Jersey from Atlanta, and Mrs. Horne passed away in June of 2008.

I am so thankful that I'd had that opportunity to live with them for that one year. It was an education and such a wonderful experience. They both lived long lives. He was nearly ninety when he passed, so he had a long, beautiful life, and Mrs. Horne a month shy of her ninety-third birthday. When Mr. Horne died, it reminded me that yet another wonderful, black man who had greatly influenced my life had gone home to be with the Lord. I miss them both so much.

Chapter 12
The Power Multiplied

Dad and Mr. Westry Horne used the multiplication of power years later to help me. I made the decision to leave my job at *Business Week* and move to Atlanta to live with my former college roommate Kathy Wilson and her family.

Dad and Mr. Horne called as many of their contacts as they could to let them know I was coming to Atlanta. Mr. Horne was a graduate of Clark Atlanta University. I compiled a very long list of contact people that they knew.

Ultimately, one of their friends, Ron Lewis, knew the publisher at the *Atlanta Journal-Constitution* (AJC), Jay Smith. After being in Atlanta for a few months and doing temporary jobs, I landed an interview at the AJC, thanks to Jay Smith, and ultimately thanks to Dad, Mr. Horne, and Ron Lewis. I interviewed with a wonderful man named Chet Fuller, the newsroom personnel manager. I thought it was interesting that he had my dad's name. He was great.

The interview went well, and I later got a call that the editor of the paper, Ron Martin, needed an assistant. His longtime secretary, Fran, had suffered a heart attack and would not be returning to work. I went in and interviewed with Ron and liked him right away. He was soft spoken, but he was sharp and had very kind eyes. We clicked. I was offered the job and snapped it up. It was a similar position to the one I'd had at *Business Week*, except, this time, I'd be working for only one person and he was the editor of the entire paper. I was essentially an editorial assistant, a glorified secretary if you will.

But Ron understood that I had a college degree, and I told him on that interview that my goal was to be a writer. He looked me in the eye and told me he had a former assistant, Wanda Lloyd, who had gone on to be the managing editor at United Press International (UPI). He had helped many people before, and if I gave him one and a half years, he would help me reach my goal.

I learned so much working for Ron. Sure, I typed letters and made appointments, but he also encouraged me to write for the company newsletter, called *The Headliner*. I wrote many articles for that publication and in the process, got to know many of the writers and editors at the paper. I also began writing for the extra zoned editions of the paper. A young man named Milton Giddens took me under his wing and regularly allowed me to write stories for *City Life*, an extra edition of the *Atlanta Journal-Constitution*. He was the sports editor of that section.

I would show the stories to Ron, and he'd put a note on it, saying something like, "Great job. Keep up the great work."

Milton later died of stomach cancer in his thirties and it was a very tough time losing a friend and colleague so young. But, I'll never forget how instrumental he was in my career.

After working for Ron for about one and a half years, I started getting a little frustrated. I enjoyed my work, but I was ready to write a lot more. I came home from work one day, and I said to my roommate, "I don't get the opportunity to write that much." She said, essentially, "Last time I checked that wasn't your job description." Kathy, Leslie Graham, and I took a trip one weekend to Charlotte to see a Charlotte Hornets basketball game, and they encouraged me to go in and speak to my boss about the promise he'd made me.

When we returned from Charlotte, I did just that. He agreed to help me get an internship as a writer in the sports department, but told me I had to sink or swim, it'd be up to me.

My mentor was J. C. Clemons, a wonderful writer and editor, who took me under his wing and really showed me the ropes. J. C. was tough, but he was just what I needed. I worked very, very hard, and he worked hard to ensure that I got the lessons that I needed. J. C. let me know that he cared about me as a person as well. He always looked out for my best interest. To this day, he is still someone I stay in touch with and consider to be a friend.

They didn't go easy on me. I had some tough assignments. I did quite a bit of enterprise work and many other challenging stories over those three months. Glenn Hannigan was the sports editor at that time. I'd like to say that I swam pretty well.

When it was all said and done, I went back to Ron. Initially, it seemed he wanted me to come back to work for him. I told him that things had gone very well in sports and that I felt like I had met every challenge. I didn't think there was any way I could go back to doing what I had been doing. I was offered a full time sports writing job there and that was the beginning of my writing career.

I ended up staying at the *Atlanta Journal-Constitution* for eight years, covering everything from high school sports, to college football, to women's pro and college basketball, and a lot of things in between. A great highlight was covering women's basketball at the 1996 Olympic Games, which were held in Atlanta. I also covered several women's NCAA (National Collegiate Athletic Association) Final Four events, including when my alma mater, UNC, defeated Louisiana Tech for the 1994 title in Richmond.

My days at the *Atlanta Journal-Constitution* were some of the best times in my career. I met so many great people, who were all willing to give a helping hand, everyone from Milton, to J. C., to Ernie Reese, to Ron Martin to Chet Fuller.

I will never forget my days in Atlanta and I will never forget how dad and Mr. Horne were directly responsible for me getting my job there.

I left Atlanta in 1998 and moved home to accept a position as a sportswriter at the *Courier-Post* in Cherry Hill, New Jersey, where I got the chance to fulfill a childhood dream; I was the Philadelphia 76ers beat writer. My dad was already gone at that point, but boy would he have been proud.

Chapter 13
The Call

Before he left earth, Daddy answered "The Call." As I said earlier, he used to have preaching contests with other kids out in the country when he was a little boy. He and his brother spent time out on the farm when they were younger, helping to pick the tobacco. My dad and the others used to pass time by having preaching contests. It's funny, he did not become a preacher until he was sixty-one. I guess he had to take care of other things that he needed to do before he heeded the call, a call he may have had since he was a boy.

When Dad when finally answered the call, Reverend Art Lewis asked him what took him so long because he had been doing this all of his life and had started talking about it when he was a member at Second Baptist Church. My dad said that he finally surrendered and gave up to the call.

Chester Whittaker, my dad, on the day he preached his "trial sermon" at St. John Baptist Church, Camden, N.J., March 26, 1995. Reverend Silas M. Townsend is at the podium.

Dad loved people, period. I think relating to people was one of his calls in life. But there was another call on his life, the ministry.

It was in his blood anyway. Uncle Clarence said my dad had a passion for preaching and for attending church since he was a young boy and that he probably inherited it from Granddaddy Roswell, who was a Baptist minister. Dad also loved going to church at Bethlehem Baptist Church in Tarboro, North Carolina, which both sides of our family have attended since the 1800's. Our family members had served (and still do serve) as assistant pastor, trustees, mother of the church, deacons, etc. This experience instilled the desire to be a minister in him.

Dad had been heavily involved in church at Second Baptist Church in Moorestown when Reverend Dr. Dennis E. Norris was the pastor. The first

Chester Whittaker, my dad, speaking or preaching at a church years before he answered his call to the ministry.

lady of the church was sister Joan Norris, a wonderful lady. We had grown up with their children, Natalie and Jean, and later, they adopted a son named Rowan. We were all so proud when Jeannie, as we called her, became part of an R&B group called Zhané that had a great deal of success with several albums which they put out. When we heard hear her songs on the radio, we beamed with pride. It was like she was a member of the family. Years later, Reverend and Mrs. Norris had a little boy named Dennis. They were great people, and we loved them dearly.

We grew up in that church, and not to be cliché, but our parents didn't send us to church, they took us. Sunday school and church were the norm every Sunday. Afterwards, we went to Nannie's house for Sunday dinner.

Chester Whittaker, my dad, and Reverend Dr. Dennis E. Norris at Princeton Theological Seminary, Princeton, New Jersey, in 1979, when Reverend Norris received his doctorate.

Dad was very close to Reverend Norris. Reverend Norris often tells a story about a misunderstanding he and Dad who was the building fund chairman and the chairman of the trustee board, among other things, once had while at Second Baptist. Dad talked to Reverend Norris on a particular Sunday morning and told him he wanted to make an announcement in front of the church. He looked up into the pulpit and apologized to Reverend Norris in front of the entire congregation. Reverend Norris said this about Dad's apology:

> I thought that was simply the greatness of your dad. I accepted that apology. He and I had been friends in addition to the fact that I was his pastor and he was a church leader. We had been personal friends through it all.

However, after Reverend Norris left to accept a position with the Cleveland Baptist Association, it wasn't very long before Mom and Dad left Second Baptist Church, and that was a huge move. That was my mom's childhood church. She'd married our dad in that church, and all of us girls were baptized in that church. We'd participated in the choirs, and done holiday plays there. It was a special place, there on the corner of Mill and Beech Streets in Moorestown.

But they left and joined St. John Baptist Church in Camden, New Jersey, under the leadership of Rev. Dr. Silas M. Townsend, a fantastic, gifted man in his own right. Dad became a deacon in the church and he also served as the director of the St. John Christian Youth Development Center.

It was at St. John that Dad finally answered the call to ministry. He approached Reverend Townsend, and told him that he'd answered the call. A book my sister Anna had shared with him one Christmas about God breaking you before he can use you had really hit home with him as well.

He went down to Newport News, and met with his "momma and daddy" and they gave their approval. He said they told him he'd been a "good boy all the days of his life" and to "preach the word" and that they supported him "150 percent."

Reverend Townsend discussed my Dad's decision to accept the call:

> It's always been clear to me when he started the struggle that the Lord was going to win and that the Lord actually had a calling on his life to preach. Something he struggled with because of his own perception that it was kind of a late in life call. He wanted to be very clear that he was doing what God would have him to do as

opposed to something that was of his own creation.

I think one of the wonderful things was his great, I would say, sensitivity to the calling process. That it was something beyond, but something that his parents certainly would recognize and others would affirm. I told him most preachers that are called know struggle. It wasn't something that was unusual. Because of his age, I think that was his greatest struggle. I always say he came to the kingdom for such a time as this. He came at the right time.

Dad had his trial sermon on March 26, 1995, at St. John Baptist Church, and we were all there. Soon after, Pastor Townsend approached dad about taking over the senior praise service on Wednesday afternoons at the church. He readily accepted that assignment.

Reverend Townsend was delighted that my dad exercised fully his gift and his ministry. He said that "Paul tells us, 'We have to make full proof of our ministry.'" Dad was able to pursue his ministry in a short period of time, and was able to get it done. Reverend Townsend explained that the senior praise service and preaching every week was a challenge. Of course, as usual, my Dad was up for the challenge, and the Reverend was glad that he accepted it. Once Dad got into it, he loved it.

Dad had his zeal for preaching, particularly for the senior praise service at the church, and his passion for people. He had a passion for getting things done properly. He was a stickler for things being done decently and in order. Reverend Townsend remembered his great capacity to organize and direct and plan and said that Dad was an incredible administrator. He was the first administrator of our Christian Youth Development Center. Besides that, he was an incredible leader and friend.

Pastor Townsend and Dad were friends before Mom and Dad joined St. John. Dad, as Mom said, always had an affinity for preachers, probably dating back to his childhood when his granddaddy was a preacher. When describing their friendship, Reverend Townsend said Dad was a very loyal friend and if Dad was in your corner, he was solidly in your corner. This quality was a comfort to the reverend and his family."

I remembered how Dad spoke at his first sermon about waking up, sometimes in the middle of the night, and hearing the call. He had also been having some health issues, as well. While I was in college, he had a warning stroke, a transient ischemic attack (TIA), and ever since, he had a small blood clot on his brain.

In more recent years, he'd been getting some headaches, in his regular routine and as he preached about. When the doctors checked it all out, there was that spot there; but it hadn't changed, or moved, so it was status quo.

His first sermon was entitled, The Before and After, talking about change. He spoke about the woman with the blood issue, and the blind man, who was made to see by Jesus. He talked about healing, and second chances.

He talked about how when you've been saved, that people should be able to tell by the way you're living your life what a wonderful change has come over you. In other words, you shouldn't be acting the same exact way you did prior to becoming saved. You shouldn't react to things in the same manner. You might be tempted to, but if you continue to keep the same company and do the same exact things you were doing prior to becoming saved, then change hasn't necessarily taken place.

It was a moving sermon, and he had quite a turnout. Reverend Norris was present the day my dad had his trial sermon. Mr. and Mrs. Horne who had been friends of my dad's for many years came down from Plainfield, New Jersey. My uncle Clarence was there. Uncle Fate Kearney came from Washington, D.C.

Uncle Clarence felt that my dad had always wanted to be a preacher, but he seemed to lose interest at one time. However, after joining Reverend Norris' church he seemed to become more serious about it. He said that Dad knew that my mom, my sisters, and I were supportive of this endeavor. Dad also mentioned that fact in his trial sermon. Uncle Clarence believed that this was a dream that finally came true for Dad.

It was also my twenty-ninth birthday, as I said, March 26, 1995. It was a joyous day. I didn't even care that it was my birthday. That day belonged completely to my dad. Deservedly so. We were all so proud. We had a get-together at the house, and I remember my mom's father, Granddaddy Young, being there. It was wonderful to have so many friends and family members together for such a positive occasion.

Mom knew that my dad "loved being in the church." She confirmed that he always became fond of the ministers that were in the church. When Dad and Mom got married, he joined Second Baptist Church because Mom was a member. He and Reverend David Minus became very close friends.

Of course Mom knew that Dad enjoyed working in the church and told about his involvement at St. John Baptist Church.

> As soon as we joined St. John's, he became involved right away. He enjoyed working at the center and he enjoyed being a deacon. He wasn't a deacon that long before he got called to the ministry. I guess it shouldn't have surprised me

because he always enjoyed preaching. He used to preach out in the fields when he was a young boy. He loved to speak. He was always well prepared. He used to get his little speeches together. He knew what he was talking about. He enjoyed crowds. He never hesitated. Some people say 'I'm getting so nervous because I have to speak or preach.' Never.

I really wondered why he went in preaching so late in life, I really think he had accomplished everything in life that he had wanted to. He lived life to the fullest, that's for sure. Not too many people can say, 'What else could I have done that I really wanted to do?' I think that was the one thing that he hadn't accomplished that he wanted to do."

When Dad preached his first sermon, many of the ministers that he knew were there. He just took a liking to the ministers. It was something that drew him to them.

Reverend Townsend who remembered Dad's voice well said that Dad had the voice of a preacher, a "great gifted trumpet." He described dad as being articulate, with wisdom and insight. Although my dad had delivered speeches before, Reverend Townsend said that preaching "was a different sort of enterprise." He believed that Dad was certainly gifted for preaching. He had the intellectual capacity for preaching. He was kind of "enamored of Dad's voice. He had the right voice. He sounded like a preacher. He was a gifted orator."

Reverend Norris also praised dad's preaching, and his "unique voice, that was something else." He said that my dad's voice communicated with people in such a way that you would not be surprised if he got a call to preach.

Reverend Norris also talked about how Dad answered the call after he left. He was not surprised, because of where Dad "had come from and who he was as a person and as a Christian." Reverend, looking back, felt that my dad "came out of an extraordinary African-American family where his mother and father laid the foundation for his life and that of his brother." He thought about his parents and the social and spiritual atmosphere out of which he came.

Reverend Norris stressed that Dad pursued his education, was an achiever, and that whatever he attempted to get done, he achieved.

He did it well. He was personable. In the sense, that he could relate to just about any and everybody. He had that sense of joy about him that he shared freely with people. As a Christian, working in the church with other people, he simply was a leader.

Mrs. Norris remembered Dad's "contagious smile" and that he had a way of making everybody feel that everything was going to be all right, which is so true, and she recalls that deep laughter as well. She also said he took his responsibilities in the church seriously and fulfilled his obligations. Mrs. Norris also said this about Dad.

> What I liked about him, he had concerns. He wouldn't mind coming and talking to you about it and trying to get an understanding about it and get things straightened out. He was that kind of person. He definitely just loved his family. No ifs ands or buts about that. He really loved his family. He was very good-natured. He had a presence about him. He was the kind of person if he just walked into a room, you would take notice of him right away. He was just a very well-rounded person.

We are so thankful that he answered the call.

Chester Whittaker, my dad, as emcee at an event for Second Baptist Church, Moorestown, New Jersey, October 1980. Dolores Whittaker, my mom, is sitting far left.

Chapter 14
The Day

I never understood why the Christmas before Dad died, I decided to come home for two weeks. I got all my work done ahead of time and planned my December vacation for New Jersey. Usually, I didn't like to be away from Atlanta for that long, but this time, something was different.

My stay at home that Christmas was great. My family loved the holidays, and Christmas was the favorite. Mom and Dad got a huge flocked tree, and we all spent a lot of time together as a family, which was the norm for Christmas time.

On Christmas morning, it was common for us to make hot chocolate and for us to sit around, usually early in the morning, ripping our gifts open. This continued when we got older, and it was the same way that Christmas.

When Dad took me to the airport and dropped me off in his red Jeep Cherokee, I actually got tears in my eyes when he pulled away. And as the airplane raced down the runway for takeoff, I cried pretty hard. It was January of 1997, and maybe in my heart, I knew that was the last Christmas holiday I would have with my dad.

I remember the day like it was yesterday. I was asleep at my apartment in Norcross, Georgia, just outside of Atlanta, when my phone rang, early one July morning. It was a Sunday. It was my mom calling to tell me that my dad had endured a bad night.

Four days earlier, he had heart bypass surgery. He was at a local hospital in New Jersey, near my hometown, Willingboro. My sister Anna and I had just returned to Atlanta the day before from a nearly two-week unexpected stay at home due to Dad's heart trouble. We had originally planned to go home for about three days, because we were having a bridal shower for Anna who was to be married in a few months.

But those three days turned into about ten days, once dad suffered a "minor" heart attack right before we got home. When he made it through the surgery, we all breathed a collective sigh of relief. He made it, he really made it. He seemed so relieved as well.

We left New Jersey, we thought, with him in pretty decent shape. But maybe he did know otherwise. I remember that Saturday when we kissed him goodbye in the hospital, how he whispered very clearly, "Remember whose hands you're in, remember who's got you covered." Not thinking it would be the last conversation I had with him, I thought he was talking about our impending flight back to Atlanta. But it wasn't meant to be. As we found out, our elation was soon deflation. In less than twenty-four hours, my dad, my hero, was dead, and we buried him later that month.

I remember my sister, Michelle (Shelly), calling back that fateful Sunday, after we'd talked to my mom, and telling me we needed to come home. Dad wasn't gone yet, but things didn't sound good.

When Shelly called, I was at my apartment in Norcross, Georgia, and a sad feeling swept over me. Sure, I had faith, but something told me that my dad was not going to be okay. It just didn't sound right that things were going down hill so fast. It all seemed so surreal that we could be talking about my strong, handsome father. Not Chester M. Whittaker. He couldn't be leaving us.

Memories came flooding back. I thought about him becoming a preacher. I thought about that voice he had. I thought about what a great Dad he had been to all of us. I thought about my mom.

My good friend Sharon Byrd rushed over to my apartment and encouraged me. I went into my bedroom and dropped to my knees and prayed for

Dolores and Chester Whittaker, my mom and dad, headed out to a social event in the 1990s. They enjoyed attending functions.

the Lord to watch over my dad. "Please Lord," I begged, "Don't let him die." I kneeled on the side of my bed and just prayed to God that my dad would be okay, that he'd make it through it. I wept for a long time, because, again, something told me that he would not. I think, in a way, my grieving process started even before my dad actually left this earth.

On the airplane ride back home to New Jersey that fateful Sunday, Anna had a vision of seeing angels around his hospital bed. She thought they were there to protect him, when, in fact, they were probably there to help carry him "home."

Anna and I flew back to Philadelphia International Airport and were met at baggage claim by her friend, Sherri Kyle, and our youngest sister, Monica. I'll never forget Monica's words, "Les, he didn't make it." I cried out. All of it was surreal. Chester M. Whittaker left this earth on July 20, 1997.

The medical staff did not know exactly what happened. The nurses said he had eaten a full breakfast that Sunday morning, July 20, 1997. Yet he ended up in cardiac arrest. Did he begin choking on his food? Had he had a massive stroke? He had diabetes as well as high blood pressure, and we knew he wasn't exactly a great candidate for bypass.

Me—Celeste Whittaker, and Chester Whittaker, my dad, at our house at 65 Courtland Lane, October 1989. Photo by Dolores Whittaker, my mom.

I can't explain the pain that I felt. The emptiness. The helplessness. There was nothing that I could do. He was gone. My daddy. Our daddy. Mom's husband and the love of her life. I didn't think I would ever be able to laugh the same way again. Nothing would ever be the same.

By the time the car pulled up outside of our home, our pastor, Reverend Dr. Silas Townsend was already at the house. He prayed with us and comforted us and told us how proud Dad would be of the way we were handling it.

I have to tell you, it all felt like a dream to me, really. It was all so surreal. So many times I had come home, since relocating to Atlanta seven years prior, and Dad was always there. Now, he would never be there again.

I remember when he was in the hospital, before he even went in for surgery, someone at our church had just passed away, and Dad said, "Wouldn't it be something to have a funeral this Saturday at Church and next Saturday as well." He was speaking about his own.

It actually scared me when he said that, because Dad had always been very intuitive. (He also had the gift of discernment in being able to judge people's character. He could sum someone up pretty quickly, and often times friends of ours would bring their male friends around so Dad could meet them, because they knew his opinion meant something.)

One thing summed up how Dad was. He had his whole funeral planned and obituary written. He left his plans right on his desk before he entered the hospital. He had specific scripture he wanted read, solos he wanted sung and people that he wanted to make remarks. We only had to make some minor updates to his obituary. He even left instructions down to the type of casket he wanted, a mahogany-colored piece. He even left his insurance policies in plain view. We didn't have to search for anything. With him planning everything out, it made that part so much easier on us. That was his way.

Reverend Norris and Mrs. Norris came to the funeral, and Reverend Norris was one of several pastors who spoke that day. Dad had requested that Reverend Norris say some words at his funeral. Later, Reverend Townsend preached a wonderful eulogy. Our families were close. Reverend Norris said "some very appropriate but good things at his memorial service" and "meant all of that because of who he was."

You never imagine putting someone you love in the ground. It was all so final when the casket was lowered into the ground at Lakeview Memorial Cemetery in Cinnaminson, New Jersey. But the day passed as if it were a dream, and I know that was nothing but God. His promise is that He will never leave you nor forsake you, and He didn't. The hardest day of my life was lived in a dream state, a slight fog. But that's how I got through it, it's how we all did.

We would have made Daddy proud on the day of his funeral. We were able to carry his plans out to a "t," and we stood tall. He deserved to be celebrated in a wonderful way in a packed church, and he was. He had made all of us so proud over the years.

Chapter 15
Daddy's Girls Remember Him

Our family gathered at Mom's house a few days before Thanksgiving in 2006. Coincidentally, Dad's birthday was November 25, always near Thanksgiving.

Anyway, my baby sister, Monica Nelson, who is in the social work field, and her family, husband Pierre Nelson, and children Pierre ("Petey") and Amber had just arrived into town from Atlanta, where they lived at that time.

My sister Michelle "Shelly" Adderley was there with her two children—Ashley and Brianna. We talked and laughed. My sister, Anna Mitchell, and her new baby, Mackenzie, joined us later in the week.

Monica pulled out a photo album, and one of the photos she pulled out was of Dad with one of his grandchildren. She said to Shelly, "He was always there, wasn't he? Always with them." Shelly nodded in approval and said,

> I remember that Dad was such a great, great person. He was a wonderful grandfather to Ashley and Brianna, and I remember him being so proud of his grandchildren. He would take Ashley down to Atco to the little pet farm and he would just be beaming to have his granddaughter with him. I just remember that Dad had a very kind spirit. He would get mad sometimes at some little things, but he had a very kind spirit. He had a deep voice and he would get your attention, but he had such a gentle heart.

Asked what she missed the most, she said,

> I miss his guidance. I miss the fact that he would give you words of wisdom. Even though sometimes you might not want to hear it, he was always right about different things. He had a good perspective on life and an outlook. I take a lot from him as far as living each day to your fullest capacity, because your days aren't promised. Dad had the attitude that you can't take it with you as far as money was concerned, and I agree.

Above: Chester Whittaker, my dad, with baby Brianna Audrey McDaniels, my niece, on the day she was born, September 9, 1994. Photo by Dolores Whittaker, my mom. Below: Chester Whittaker with his first grandchild, Ashley Adderley, November 1991. Photo by Michelle Adderley, my sister.

Monica who is the youngest daughter had many special memories of Dad, remembering that "he was there for all my firsts." He was there for the birth of her first child, Amber. He walked her down the aisle at her wedding. He actually gave her diploma to her at her college graduation at Richard Stockton State College, and he also spoke at the graduation. She is blessed to be the only one of us to say that Dad not only handed her diploma to her, but was the commencement speaker at her graduation. What a memory for her! He was there when she bought her first home and gave her the last bit of money she needed for the purchase. He helped her get her first job out of college.

Monica (née Whittaker) Nelson, my sister, and Chester Whittaker, my dad, on her wedding day, October 15, 1994.

Dad also had a very special relationship with Anna. Anna was so much like him. They were both born under the sign of Sagittarius and were both outgoing and outspoken.

I remember once when Anna and her boyfriend had split up in college when she was at the University of Delaware. On Valentine's Day, dad drove to Delaware and took Anna flowers and also gave her a necklace along with a card. He knew she was grieving the relationship and wanted to do something to make her feel better.

I jokingly told my mom, "none of the rest of us got anything for Valentine's Day from Dad." But, I also knew that Anna held a special place in his heart, as we all did, and that he knew she needed the extra attention at that time.

Anna shared a story, too, which sums up the way Dad was. She was about eight-years-old and was home from school due to being sick. Dad had an important affair to attend at Governor Brendan Byrne's mansion. He took his little girl along. Anna explained why this was important:

> Here's another small example of how Dad prepared us for
> the real world. Dad was working for the governor of New

Dolores Whittaker, my mom, Anna Whittaker, my sister, and Chester Whittaker, my dad, at her college graduation at the University of Delaware, January 1991.

Jersey at the time and instead of trying to find a relative to take care of me, he took me to the Governor's mansion with him. It was during the Christmas holidays and there was a party going on at the mansion that day. I was the only child at the party, and I felt out of place for that reason. I'm sure there were very few blacks in the room, but that's not what I remember. I didn't feel out of place because of the color of my skin, only because I was a child. That was how I was raised. I didn't focus on color and to this day many times I don't even realize when I am the only brown face in the room.

Somehow, I knew that my dad belonged in that room with those people, many of whom were probably much more wealthy and connected than we were, but you wouldn't have known it based on how Dad carried himself. I just remember everything being so big to me, including Dad, as I followed him around the main room where the party was being held.

Travis, Mackenzie, Anna, and Myles Mitchell, my brother-in-law, niece, sister, and nephew, at home in Lawrenceville, Georgia, July 27, 2007. Photo by Dolores Whittaker.

Anna said she doesn't remember a whole lot from her childhood but that particular day has stayed with her all these years.

> I think that maybe I was proud of him, but just didn't even know it. I didn't understand what I was feeling at the time, but I wish I could go back to that day now with all that I know. Dad never let anyone make him feel less than and this is something he passed down to me and I try to instill that same sense of pride in my children.

He also always seemed to know just what to do. Unfortunately, he died two months before Anna wed her Travis (Mitchell). The wedding took place at Second Baptist Church in Moorestown. And while it was a tough day (I, admittedly, sobbed when I saw Anna being walked down the aisle by Uncle Clarence, who looked so much like Dad), knowing Dad wasn't there to walk her down the aisle, we knew he was looking down on us. He was so looking forward to Anna's wedding day, and had said in the hospital that, hopefully, by the time she got married, he would be in good enough shape to walk her down the aisle.

Chester Whittaker, my dad, and Saundra Umstead-Capers, my oldest sister, in December 1986. Photo by the author.

My oldest sister, Saundra, did make it to the wedding. As I said earlier, Dad and Saundra's mom divorced when Saundra was a little girl, so unfortunately, we didn't get the chance to grow up with her.

But Dad would be so happy that we've all gotten closer over the last few years. I ran into Saundra at Starbucks (one of my favorite places), in Moorestown, the very town where my mom and my dad met.

She was with her daughter Emerald. Saundra and I talked and hugged and exchanged phone numbers. Emerald looked so much like Shelly that it was uncanny. Saundra had entered the special education field, like Dad. That day, we reconnected. Since then, we have spoken on the phone regularly, and Emerald and Jackie, Saundra's daughter who she adopted, have spent time at my house and at Shelly's house, as well. Brianna, Shelly's youngest daughter, Emerald, and Jackie get along well and the three have spent the night at each others' houses. Saundra had us over for dinner on numerous occasions, and she even visited Anna and Monica when they lived in Atlanta, Georgia. (Monica and Anna have moved back to New Jersey).

It's a shame Dad didn't get to know Saundra the way he wanted to when she was young, but I'm thankful they got to know each other better later in his life.

Chapter 16
The Grands

Ashley Nicole Adderley was born on May 5, 1989. I remember the day so well. I knew my sister, Shelly, had gone into labor. I had gone out to lunch at my job at *Business Week*, and when I returned, there was a note on my desk. "Your sister had the baby: It's a girl." I wept.

Ashley was all of our pride and joy, but none more than my dad. He had his first grandchild, and he was so proud. He loved that little girl so much. Mom said,

> Ashley was the joy of his life, really. That was his first grand-child. He just thought so much of her. That was his heart. We'd go over there in the morning and put her on the bus. He always looked out for Shelly. He just felt responsible for her because of the fact that she didn't have a husband at that time.

I remember that he would put a little sign on his red Jeep, "Ashley's Bus." He'd pick her up and drop her off at school like it was nothing. Anything she needed, he would buy it for her. She was the apple of his eye.

Ashley Nicole Adderley, my niece, with her daughter Aliyah, 2008.

When Brianna Audrey McDaniels was born on Sept. 9, 1994, Dad was just as happy, and soon after Amber Monet Nelson, Monica and Pierre's first baby, was born on July 6, 1996. My mom, who also just adores all of her grandkids, watched all of the kids when they were babies. I remember how excited my dad would get when the kids would get dropped off in the morning. He'd come racing down the steps.

Before Dad died he didn't get the chance to know my sister Saundra's daughter Emerald, who is one year older than Bri, but he did want to know her. Dad loved Saundra very much, even though after he divorced her mom, he didn't get the opportunity to spend time with her as much as he wanted to. I think it's something he regretted, because he never really got the chance to know her like he desired and vice versa.

My dad never got the chance to see his first grandson, my nephew, Pierre Nelson, who we called "Petey." Monica's baby boy was something else. I had the chance to see him delivered on June 14, 1998, along with my sister Shelly and Monica's husband Pierre. It was a miracle watching the birth happen.

Chester Whittaker's legacy of grandchildren. Above: Saundra Umstead-Capers, my oldest sister, and her daughter, Emerald Capers, August 2009 in Miami, Florida. Below: Brianna A. McDaniels, Pierre "Petey" Nelson, with his sister, Gabrielle Nelson, on his lap, Amber M. Nelson. Opposite page, above: Myles and Mackenzie Mitchell, June 2008; below: Pierre Nelson, my brother-in-law, and Gabrielle Nelson, April 2008.

The next grandchild was Myles Quinton Mitchell, Anna's son, who was born on Sept. 15, 2000, and then Mackenzie Danielle Mitchell, Myles' little sister, would come along on Feb. 7, 2006. Last, but not least, Monica and Pierre's baby girl, Gabrielle Nicole Nelson, was born on June 6, 2007. What a blessing.

Mom and Dad's very first great-grandchild, Ashley's daughter, Aliyah Nichelle Adderley, was born on January 15, 2008. This was meaningful to the family, since January 15 was the same day that the late Rev. Dr. Martin Luther King, Jr., was born.

They are all beautiful, loving, caring children, and they are the kind of kids my dad would've doted on. They are kind and smart and funny. They all love family.

Remember kids, your granddad and great-granddad loved you so much (even the ones he never got the chance to meet), and he would have been so proud of you. You are all very special and unique, and you can be anything that you want to be in life. Just work hard and put your trust and faith in God.

Chapter 17
Remember Whose
Hands You're In

I guess I'm still grieving, really, all these years later. You see, you don't lose someone that was that much a part of your life and existence and ever forget them. I remember the Monday morning after he passed, waking up and thinking, for the first time in my life, I no longer had a father. It felt like someone had punched me very hard in the stomach, and I wept some more.

You never stop missing your dad. You never stop loving him. You just adapt and adjust and you learn to go on without them, but it's not easy. There is not a day that goes by that I don't think about my dad.

He truly was my hero. You see, a hero is not someone that has to be perfect. You don't have to look at them as a god, who has no chinks in his or her armor. My dad was human, and he bled and wept and hurt just like everyone else.

But, he was my hero because he was real. He was smart, loyal, loving, and trusting and honest. He was all those things and more.

One of the greatest gifts he and my mom gave to me and my sisters was a belief and trust in the Lord. When Dad told me on that Saturday afternoon before he died (on Sunday) to remember whose hands I was in, I never forgot that.

That simple phrase actually let me know in advance, that no matter what happened, everything was going to be all right. Because God not only had my dad covered, but he had all of us covered as well.

The Lord loves us so much. When we were little girls at Second Baptist Church, we had to memorize scriptures in Sunday school, and I remember learning John 3:16. It says, "For God so loved the world that He gave His only begotten son and whosoever believeth in Him shall not perish, but have everlasting life." That simple scripture will help you get through so many trials in life. When you think about how much God loves us and you understand that He has already paid the price for the atonement of our sins, you understand that everything will be all right.

When you think about His grace and His mercy and His love, it makes life bearable, no matter the circumstances.

You also think about the fact that His only begotten son was sent here to live among us. He was birthed from Virgin Mary's womb, he came into this world like every one of us has come into this world: out of a woman. He felt what we feel. He felt pain, he felt sickness, he felt betrayal. All the things we go through, He went through. Then came that fateful day where He was beaten badly, then suffered horribly on that cross on a hill called Calvary because that was His purpose in life.

On that day when he was near his end he looked up to the heavens and said, "It is finished." He came in the flesh so he could die for our sins. That is love. That is real love.

You also realize that if Jesus Christ, the son of God, can go through pain and suffer and have trials and tribulations, then God is certainly not promising us that we won't go through our share of it on Earth.

So while we went through some trying times after Daddy's death, God was our blanket throughout. He sent the comforter and enveloped us all with a wall of protection. He had us covered all the while.

Daddy was right.

Chester Whittaker, my dad, with four of his five daughters, me—Celeste, Anna, Michelle (Shelly), and Monica on Shelly's high school graduation day in 1982. Photo by Dolores Whittaker, my mom.

Epilogue
The Epitome of Fatherhood

Gregarious. Boisterous. A great orator. Generous. Intelligent. Sports lover. Supportive. Dependable. A leader. Independent. A chef. Family man. Child of God. Open. A teacher.

You are so many different things. A diversified man for sure. You're the one that always gets things done, and for problems you quite often have the cure.

Through the years, you've been a constant like sunshine or rain. We didn't always understand, but as time passed, our ignorance waned. You are the epitome of fatherhood, about this there is no question. We could always come to you with any thoughts or even silly suggestions.

Anytime trouble came knocking, you were there to answer the door. And at our concerts and basketball games you were the loudest cheerleader on the floor.

So, Dad, tonight is your night. A special one indeed. We just wanted to take the time to say we love you, and thanks for being there in our many times of need!

C. E. W. (written in 1988)

Bibliography

Adderley, Michelle. Personal interview with author, June 2007.

Alpha Phi Alpha Fraternity, Inc. "About Alpha: History; An Alpha Legacy: The Founding Jewels," Alpha Phi Alpha Fraternity, Inc., http://www. alpha-phi-alpha.com/ (accessed March 2009).

Barber, Bill. "Former Burlington Track Coach Coaching Others," *Burlington County Times*, October 24, 1968.

Bodall, Thomas C. *Salient Facts: N.J. State Home for Boys.* Jamesburg Historical Association, http://www.jamesburghistory.com (digitalized 6/3/2006) (accessed July 2009).

Ewing Township Board of Education. "Antheil Elementary School," Ewing Township, New Jersey, Board of Education, http://www.ewing.k12. nj.us/EwingWeb/Schools/Antheil/antheilhome.html (accessed July 2009).

Giordano, Paul. "Whittaker's resignation made official," *Burlington County Times*, May 22, 1965.

Historic Burlington City, New Jersey. "William R. Allen School," Historic Burlington City, New Jersey, http://08016.com/allen-school.html (accessed July 2009).

HistoryMakers. "Adam Wade Biography," *HistoryMakers,* http://www. thehistorymakers.com/biography/biography.asp?bioindex=1686&cate gory=EntertainmentMakers&occupation=Singer%2C%20Actor%20 %26%20Director&name=Adam%20Wade (accessed September 2009).

Horne, Westry. Personal conversation with author, December 2001, and with Art Lewis, phone interview, 2007.

Jones, Doris. Letter to author, March 22, 2009.

Lewis, Art. Telephone interview with author, March 7, 2007.

Lurie, Maxine N. and Marc Mappen, eds. "Prisons." *The Encyclopedia of New Jersey.* Rutgers University Press, 2004, pp. 661-662.

Lyons, Clarkie. Letter to author, March 19, 2009.

Mitchell, Anna. Personal interview with author and email, March 27, 2009.

Nelson, Monica. Personal interview with author, June 2007.

New Jersey State Legislature, Office of Legislative Services, Office of the State Auditor. *Juvenile Justice Commission: Juvenile Medium Security Center,* July 1, 1998, to June 7, 2000.

Newport News, Virginia. "Welcome to the City of Newport News." Newport News, Virginia, http://www.nngov.com/ (accessed March 2008).

————. "Facts and Figures," Newport News, Virginia, http://www. newport-news.org/media-center/newport-news-in-detail/facts-and-figures.html (accessed July 2009).

Newport News Public Schools, Huntington Middle School. "Our School: About Our School," Newport News Public Schools, http://huntington. nn.k12.va.us (accessed July 2009).

Norris, Dennis E. Telephone interview with author, May 30, 2007.

Norris, Joan. Telephone interview with author, May 30, 2007.

Richardson, Eula. Telephone interview with author, March 2007.

Tarboro, North Carolina. "The Official Town of Tarboro, North Carolina Web Site," Tarboro, North Carolina, http://www.tarboro-nc.com, (accessed March 2008).

Townsend, Silas. Telephone interview with author, April 15, 2007.

U.S. Army, Fort Dix. "About Fort Dix: History; John Adams Dix and the history of Fort Dix," U.S. Army, Fort Dix, http://www.dix.army.mil/ history/history.htm (accessed July 2009).

Vineland, New Jersey. Vineland Archives Alive. "The Vineland Training School: People; Edward R. Johnstone," Vineland, New Jersey, http:// www.vineland.org/history/trainingschool/people/johnstone.htm (accessed July 2009).

Whitaker, Chester Sr. Personal interview and conversation with author, February 2004.

Whitaker, Hazel. Personal conversation with author, April 1994.

Whittaker, Chester M. Scrapbook, September 1991.

————. Funeral program insert of remarks at Birt Whitaker's funeral, Feb. 24, 1995.

Whittaker, Clarence. E-mail interview with author, March 5, 2007.

Whittaker, Dolores. Personal interview with author, June 2007.

Index

A

Adderley, Aliyah Nichelle 80
Adderley, Ashley Nicole 27, 69, 77
Adderley, Michelle (Shelly) Yvonne (née Whittaker) 15, 20, 27, 29, 64, 77
  memories of father 69
  wedding 33
Adderley, Sara 33
Allen, Arrillear (née Kearney) 6
Allen, Ray 6
Alley, Jennifer 34
Alpha Phi Alpha Fraternity, Inc. 8–9, 47
Anderson, Doris 37
Atlanta Journal-Constitution (AJC) 51–53
Aunt Liz. *See* Whittaker, Elizabeth (née Smith)
Aunt Sister. *See* Brown, Florence
Aunt Teentsy. *See* Allen, Arrillear (née Kearney)

B

basketball 4, 7, 9, 11, 21–23, 27, 33, 34–38
Bethlehem Baptist Church (Tarboro, N.C.)
  Whitaker and Kearney families 56
Bethune, Mary McLeod 48
Bo. *See* Whitaker, Royster Leon
Brother Bill. *See* Whitaker, Royster Leon
Brown, Florence 5, 30
Brown, Theodore 5
Brown, William 5
Bubba. *See* Brown, Theodore
Burlington County Times (Burlington, N.J.) 17, 42–43
BusinessWeek (magazine) 35, 38, 47
Butler, Kim 23
Byrd, Sharon 48, 64
Byrne, Brendan (N.J. governor) 42, 72–73

C

Camp Lejeune (N.C.) 6
Carter, Claude 30
Clark Atlanta University (Atlanta, Ga.) 51
Clemons, J. C. 52–53
Cleveland Baptist Association (Ohio) 58

Collis Porter Huntington High School. *See* Virginia; Newport News; Huntington High School
Cornell University 8
Courier-Post (Camden, N.J.) 21, 53
Cousin Sis. *See* Richardson, Eula (née Kearney)

D

Dada. *See* Young, Albert H., Sr.
Dallas, Margie (née Young) 12

E

Edward R. Johnstone Training and Research Center (Bordentown, N.J.) 25
Erving, Julius ("Dr. J") 21
Evans, N. Dean 25

F

Fisk University (Nashville, Tn.) 3
Fort Dix (N.J.) 11, 25
Fuller, Chet 51, 53

G

Georgia
  Atlanta 9, 35, 49–51, 51–53, 63, 66, 69, 75
  Norcross 63
Giddens, Milton 51
Glassboro State College (N.J., now Rowan University) 13–14
Graham, Leslie 52
Granddaddy Roswell. *See* Whitaker, Rev. Roswell

H

Hannigan, Glenn 52
Hicks, Margaret (née Young) 33
Horne, Dorothy 48–49, 60
Horne, Jackie 48
Horne, Judi 48
Horne, Westry 47–49, 60
Huntington High School. *See* Virginia; Newport News; Huntington High School

I

Illinois 19–20
  Evanston 20
  Northfield 19

J

Jackson, Maynard 9
Jobes family (in Newport News, Virginia) 8
Jones, Doris (née Lyons) 5

K

Kearney, Annabelle 31–32
Kearney, Dock
  Whittaker family visits to his farm 31–32
Kearney, Earl, Jr. 32
Kearney, Earl, Sr. 32
Kearney, Eula (née Whitaker) 5
Kearney, Fate 4, 45, 60
Kearney, Gary 32
Kearney, Lewis 4, 32
Kearney, Richard 5
Kearney, William 5–6
Kimbrough, Rev. Casey 46
King, Rev. Dr. Martin Luther, Jr. 9, 20, 80
Kyle, Sherri 65

L

Lewis, Art 43, 55
Lewis, Ron 51
Lloyd, Wanda 51
Lucas, Anna 14
Lyons, Clarkie (née Whitaker) 1, 5

M

Manual Training and Industrial School for Colored Youth (Bordentown, N.J.) 25
Marquis, Milton 26
Marshall, Thurgood 9
Martin, Barbara (Mrs. Clarence) 28
Martin, Clarence 28
Martin, Doug 28
Martin, Michael 28
Martin, Ron 51–52
  his secretary Fran 51
Maryland
  Baltimore 32
  Glen Burnie 31
McDaniels, Brianna Audrey 69
Minus, Rev. David 60
Mitchell, Anna Catherine (née Whittaker) 16–18, 20, 28, 29, 33–34, 58, 65, 69, 73, 75
  college graduation day 72
  memories of father 72–74
Mitchell, Mackenzie Danielle 69, 73, 78–79
Mitchell, Myles Quinton 73, 78–79
Mitchell, Travis 73, 74

Morgan State College (Baltimore, Md.) 8

N

Nannie. *See* Young, Margie (née Gale)
National Collegiate Athletic Association (NCAA) 52
Nelson, Amber Monet 69, 78
Nelson, Gabrielle 78–79
Nelson, Monica Leigh (née Whittaker) 19–20, 20, 29, 33–34, 69, 75
  memories of father 69, 71–72
  wedding day 71
Nelson, Pierre 69, 78–79
Nelson, Pierre ("Petey") 69, 78
New Jersey
  Burlington City
    Burlington City High School 16
    William R. Allen School 11, 25
  Burlington Township 21
    LaGorce Square 15–16, 19
  Department of Corrections
    Annandale Reformatory For Boys 42
    Bordentown Reformatory 42
    Clinton State Home for Girls 42
    Mountainview Youth Correctional Facility 42
    New Jersey State Home for Boys near Jamesburg 42
    New Jersey State Reform School 42
    New Jersey Training School for Boys 42
    Youth Correctional Facility at Bordentown 42
  Edward R. Johnstone Training and Research Center (Bordentown) 25
  Ewing Township
    William L. Antheil Elementary School 25
  Manual Training and Industrial School for Colored Youth (Bordentown) 25
  Moorestown 11–14
  Office of Economic Opportunity
    Department of Community Affairs 43
  Pemberton 26
    Pemberton High School 26
  Plainfield 48
  segregated schools 11
  Tabernacle 28
  Willingboro 21, 47, 63
    Hawthorne Park Elementary School 21
    Rancocas Valley Hospital 15
    Willingboro High School 23, 26
Newport, Christopher 2
New York

Ithaca 8
New York City 21
  World Trade Center 47
Norris, Dennis 57
Norris, Rev. Dr. Dennis E. 56, 60, 61–62
Norris, Jean 57
Norris, Joan 57, 62
Norris, Natalie 57
Norris, Rowan 57
North Carolina 23, 33–39, 56
  Camp Lejeune 6
  Edgecombe County 1
  Fayetteville 36
  Leggett 1
  Raleigh 1
  Tarboro 1, 4, 56
  Tar River 1
  University of North Carolina (Chapel Hill) 23, 33–39
  Whitakers 4

O

O'Leary, Hazel 3
Owens, Jesse 9

P

Pennsylvania
  Philadelphia 12, 21
Philadelphia 76ers 21, 53
Pilgrim Baptist Church (Newark, N.J.) 43
Police Athletic League (PAL) 21–23

R

Rancocas Valley Hospital (Willingboro, N.J.) 15
Reese, Ernie 53
Richardson, Eula (née Kearney) 5–6
Richard Stockton State College of New Jersey 46, 71
Rider College (Lawrenceville, N.J., now Rider University) 41
Roy, Bernice 11, 13

S

Sanders, J. B. 10, 33
Second Baptist Church (Moorestown, N.J.) 15, 44–46, 55, 56, 74
segregated schools 3, 11
Smith, Otis 8
  member of Alpha Phi Alpha Fraternity, Inc. 8
Smook. *See* Kearney, William

Sonny Boy. *See* Brown, William
St. John Baptist Church (Camden, N.J.) 46, 58–61

T

Taft, Timothy 36
Townsend, Rev. Dr. Silas M. 58–59, 61
Trenton State College (The College of New Jersey) 16, 41

U

Umstead-Capers, Saundra (née Whittaker) 11, 20, 75–76, 78
University of Delaware (Newark) 72
University of North Carolina (Chapel Hill) 23, 33–39

V

Virginia
  Chesapeake Bay 2
  James River 2
  Newport News 2–4, 3–5, 29, 58
    Booker T. Washington Elementary School 3
    Hampton Roads Harbor 2
    Huntington High School 3, 7
    public school system 2
    shipyard 2, 29
  Petersburg 33
  segregated schools 3
Virginia State University (Petersburg) 41

W

Wade, Adam (born Patrick Henry Wade) 9
Watkins, Shirley (née Young) 12
Whitaker and Kearney families 4, 56
Whitaker, Birt 4, 4–5
  organized preaching contests 5
Whitaker, Chester ("Sr.') 1–3, 29–31, 58
  Christian values 2
  construction skills 2
    renovates home into two-story house 3
  determined to educate sons 3
  employment
    Newport News shipyard 2, 29
    U.S. Postal Service 2, 29
  working two jobs 8
Whitaker, Hazel Lee (née Kearney) 1–3, 5, 29–31, 58
  attended public school in Edgecombe County, N.C. 1
  Christian values 2
  determined to educate sons 3

working two jobs 8
Whitaker, Jefferson 1
Whitaker, Rev. Roswell 1, 4–5
  Baptist minister 1, 3, 56
  Bethlehem Baptist Church (Tarboro, N.C.) 56
  farmer 4–5
    growing tobacco 5
    sharecropping 1
Whitaker, Royster 5, 30
Whitaker, Royster Leon 5
Whittaker, Anna Catherine. *See* Mitchell, Anna Catherine (née Whittaker)
Whittaker, Celeste Elaine 20, 29, 65
  apartment in Norcross, Georgia 64
  basketball 23, 34–38
    love of as juvenile 21–22
    Police Athletic League (PAL)
      most valuable player trophy 21–22
    practice and training 22
  birthplace 15
  career in journalism
    Atlanta Journal Constitution (Atlanta, Ga.) 35, 52
    beginning of writing career 52
    BusinessWeek magazine (New York City) 35, 38, 47–48
    Courier-Post (Cherry Hill, N.J.) 53
      sportswriter 21
  Christian beliefs 81–82
  education
    University of North Carolina, Chapel Hill 33–40
      basketball team 35–37
      full athletic scholarship for basketball 23
      graduation 38
    Willingboro High School
      basketball team all-star player 22–23
  father as hero 81
  grief over father's death 74, 81
  last Christmas holiday with dad 63
  learning to ride bike 19
  living with Horne family 48–49
  memories of father 81–82, 83
Whittaker, Chester Mack
  Association for Schools and Agencies for the Handicapped (ASAH)
    president of 43
  awards 43, 44–46
    Council on Exceptional Children's Convention (Canada)

all-expense paid trip to 44
Second Baptist Church (Moorestown, N.J.) 44
birthplace 1
brother Clarence
  close relationship with 1, 25–27, 45
call to ministry 55–62
  trial sermon (March 26, 1995) 59–60
cardiac disease and diabetes 63–67
  heart bypass surgery 63
changed spelling of last name (surname) 1–2
childhood
  early and middle years 1–3, 4
  teen years 3–9
    playing basketball with neighborhood kids 4
Christian values
  belief in 47
coaching
  Burlington City High School 16–17
    cross country 16
    football 16
    track 16
  Celeste in basketball 21–23
  Fort Dix, N.J. 11
    baseball 11
    basketball 11
cousin Eula (née Kearney) Richardson
  close relationship with 5
death and burial
  funeral planned and obituary written 66
  interment 66
education and training
  Booker T. Washington Elementary School (Newport News, Va.) 3
  Huntington High School
    activities and awards 7
    basketball team 7
  Rider College
    school administrator certificates 41
  Trenton State College
    masters degree 41
  Virginia State College 8–10, 41
    joins Alpha Phi Alpha Fraternity, Inc. 8
    member basketball team 9
    Reserve Officers' Training Corps (ROTC) 10
    scholarship to attend from Otis Smith 8

summer job to help pay tuition 8
educator and administrator, career as
  Archway Programs
    executive director for 43
  Burlington County College (Burlington, N.J.) 42
    assistant to the president 25
    Educational Opportunity Fund Program 25
  Camden County College (Blackwood, N.J.) 44
  Edward R. Johnstone Training and Research Center (Bordentown, N.J.) 25
  National School Boards Association (Illinois) 19–20
    director of minority affairs 42
  Richard Stockton State College of New Jersey (Pomona, N.J.)
    board of trustees, member of 46
  special education 11, 16
  Trenton State College (Trenton, N.J.)
    demonstration teacher 17, 25
  William L. Antheil Elementary School (Ewing Township, N.J.) 25
  William R. Allen School (Burlington City, N.J.) 25
family values 17
first great-grandchild
  Adderley, Aliyah Nichelle 80
first marriage 11
government career
  federal 43
    Dept. of Health Education and Welfare (HEW) (N.Y. City) 43
  New Jersey
    Department of Education, N.J. Correctional Program 41
    Office of the Governor 42
grandchildren 69, 77–80
  spending time with
    Ashley Nicole Adderley 70, 77
    Brianna Audrey McDaniels 70
leadership traits 4, 8, 10–11, 16–17, 25, 43
marriage to Delores Elaine Young, date of 15
military service
  Fort Dix, New Jersey
    coaching sports teams 11
    commissioned as officer in Army 11
newspaper interviews
  Burlington County Times 17, 42–43
nicknames for family members 2, 5
personality 6, 7, 10, 14, 31, 46, 56, 62, 66, 81
  as social butterfly 33, 37
  loving to dress well 4

   tailor-made suits 10, 33
   outgoing and talkative 4, 16
   persistence in accomplishing goals 43
   risk taker 41
   sense of humor 4, 5, 6, 26
   warm and loving 4
preaching and oratorical skills 61
raising daughters 17, 20
   Anna
      college graduation day 72
      consoling on Valentine's Day 72
      taking to governor's mansion 72–73
   building self-esteem 18
   Celeste
      driving to job interview 38–39
      taking to college 33–35
      teaching about sports and taking to games 21
      teaching to ride bike 19
   church membership 58
   encouraging self-expression 20
   instilling Christian values 18
   Michelle (Shelly)
      hosting wedding of 33
   Monica
      involved in special "firsts" in her life 71
   playing sports 21
Second Baptist Church (Moorestown, N.J.)
   as trustee 46
      chairman of trustee board 58
   building fund chairman 58
   membership in 56, 60
social activities 64
   hosting parents recommitment ceremony 33
   visits to parents and other relatives 29
southern roots 31, 47
St. John Baptist Church (Camden, N.J.)
   answered call to ministry 58
   Christian Youth Development Center
      director of 58, 59
   deacon in 46, 58
   role in 60–61
striving for racial and gender equality
   as trailblazer in employment 41–42
   mentoring careers of black, women, and other minorities 47–49
   multiplication of power concept 47, 51

summers in Tarboro and Whitakers, North Carolina 4–6
  grandfather's farm
    competing in preaching contests 5, 55
    working in tobacco fields 4–5, 55
Whittaker, Clare 26–27
Whittaker, Clarence Edward, Jr. 26–27
Whittaker, Clarence Edward, Sr. 1–4, 25–28, 45, 56, 60, 74
  changed spelling of last name (surname) 2
  education
    Booker T. Washington Elementary School (Newport News, Va.) 3
    Huntington High School (Newport News, Va.) 3
    Morgan State College (Baltimore, Md.) 8
      joins Alpha Phi Alpha Fraternity, Inc. 8
  educator and administrator, career as
    Burlington County College (Burlington, N.J.)
      Educational Opportunity Fund Program 25
    Edward R. Johnstone Training and Research Center (Bordentown, N.J.) 25
    Trenton State College (Trenton, N.J.)
      demonstration teacher 25
    William L. Antheil Elementary School (Ewing Township, N.J.) 25
    William R. Allen School (Burlington City, N.J.) 25
  move to New Jersey 25
  personality 26
  recognition for accomplishments 43
Whittaker, Dolores Elaine (née Young) 12–18
  birthplace 12
  career as educator
    Burlington City (N.J.) 19
    Burlington Township (N.J.) 19
    elementary school teacher 13
    Willingboro (N.J.) 19
  childhood 12–13
  education 12–14
    Glassboro State College (N.J., now Rowan University) 13
  first great-grandchild
    Adderley, Aliyah Nichelle 80
  marriage to Chester Mack Whittaker, date of 15
  motherhood 15, 19–20
  raising daughters
    Anna
      college graduation day 72
    building self-esteem 18
    Celeste
      attending her basketball games 23
    church membership 58

encouraging self-expression 20
instilling Christian values 18
Michelle (Shelly)
  hosting wedding of 33
period as stay-at-home mom 19
Second Baptist Church (Moorestown, N.J.) 15
  childhood church 58
  membership in 60
social activities 64
  entertaining family and friends 33, 60
St. John Baptist Church (Camden, N.J.) 58
Whittaker, Elizabeth (née Smith) 26–27
Whittaker, Gina 26–27
Whittaker, Karla 26–27
Whittaker, Lisa 26
Whittaker, Michelle (Shelly) Yvonne. *See* Adderley, Michelle (Shelly) Yvonne (née
      Whittaker)
Whittaker, Monica Leigh. *See* Nelson, Monica Leigh (née Whittaker)
Whittaker, Pam 26–27
William L. Antheil Elementary School (Ewing Township, N.J.) 25
William R. Allen School (Burlington City, N.J.) 11, 16, 25, 41
Willingboro High School (Willingboro, N.J.) 23, 26
Wilson, Kathy 34, 51
Wilson, Vivian 35

Y

Young, Albert H., Jr. 12, 60
Young, Albert H., Sr. 12–14
Young, Albert (Uncle "Sonny," son of Albert Jr.) 12
Young, Andrew 9
Young, Anna Mae (née Myers) 12
Young, Darlene 12
Young, Dolores Elaine. *See* Whittaker, Dolores Elaine (née Young)
Young, James 12
Young, Kathy 12
Young, Lena 12
Young, Leroy 12
Young, Margie. *See* Dallas, Margie (née Young)
Young, Margie (née Gale) 12–14, 33
Young, Shirley. *See* Watkins, Shirley (née Young)
Young, Theodore 12

Z

Zhané (R&B group) 57

About the Author

Celeste E. Whittaker, a native of Willingboro, New Jersey, has been a sports-writer at the *Courier-Post* newspaper in Cherry Hill, New Jersey, since April 1998. During her time there, she has covered the Philadelphia 76ers basketball team, college sports, and high school sports. She previously worked at the *Atlanta Journal-Constitution* newspaper for eight years, covering women's and men's basketball, including at the 1996 Olympic Games, and college football and high school sports. Whittaker started her journalism career as an editorial assistant at *BusinessWeek* magazine in New York City.

Playing sports has also contributed to Whittaker's expertise. The South Jersey native was a scholarship basketball player at the University of North Carolina, Chapel Hill before a knee injury ended her career.

Whittaker who earned a bachelor's degree in journalism from the University of North Carolina has won several writing awards, including the New Jersey Press Association first place for sports portfolio in 2000, the Monica Kauffman Media Award in 1999, the Georgia Council on Social Welfare Journalism award in 1997, and second place in 2001 for the Garden State Association of Black Journalists Profile Award.

In her spare time, Celeste Whittaker enjoys volunteering with a literacy program, called "Bookmates." *The Epitome of Fatherhood* is is her first book.

LaVergne, TN USA
10 May 2010
182206LV00012B/180/P